"Hawkin serves hearty doses of inspiration and imagination while frequently drawing on giants of literature and philosophy . . . Vital advice for the tale spinner in each of us." —PUBLISHERS WEEKLY

"Remarkable, authentic, and enlightening . . . The drive this book instills in the reader to put these practices into play in their own lives will keep readers coming back to this book repeatedly, very much in tune with other great books like Stephen King's "On Writing." —ANTHONY AVINA

"Hawkin is refreshingly honest about her own experiences, establishing her expertise with gentle humor and humility. If writing is a journey, then Hawkin is the perfect guide to its unexplored and untamed reaches: inspiring, forthright, and inventive." —MARIE POWELL, LAST OF THE GIFTED SERIES

"An invaluable resource that empowers writers, allowing them to approach their craft with confidence . . . An essential addition to any writer's toolbox." —JOSHUA ROY

"A craft tool and spiritual journey guided by a skillful, compassionate mentor . . . Stands out from other craft books." —SIONNACH WINTERGREEN, MEN OF THE SHADOWS SERIES

BOOKS BY W. L. HAWKIN

The Hollystone Mysteries

To Charm a Killer

To Sleep with Stones

To Render a Raven

To Kill a King

To Dance with Destiny

Lure: Jesse & Hawk

Writing with your Muse: a Guide to Creative Inspiration

Writing with your Muse

A Guide to Creative Inspiration

W. L. Hawkin

BLUE HAVEN PRESS

Writing with your Muse: a Guide to Creative Inspiration

Copyright © 2023 by W. L. Hawkin

Book Cover by W. L. Hawkin

Edited by Wendy Hawkin

Author Photo by Panziera Photography

Published by Blue Haven Press

HTTP://BLUEHAVENPRESS.COM

CONTENTS

PREFACE

Inspire/Inspirare: the drawing in of breath.
"Words float on the wind. Breathe them in.
Exhale them on the page."

About This Book

Writing with your Muse offers techniques, strategies, tools, tips, and stories to help you tap into creative inspiration and get your words on the page.

Everything you'll read here is something I've explored and experienced. To date, I've written poetry, creative nonfiction, several novels, and even designed workshops using what I call my "intuitive process." My books have been described as "cinematic" because I view each scene as if it were part of a film and then choose words to describe my sensory experience.

You don't have to be psychic to be successful with these techniques, although that natural ability exists in all of us, and these techniques will help you develop your sixth sense. There's even science to back it up. Rest assured, whatever brought you here, there's a reason, and your muse is waiting to take this journey with you. This book will help if:

- you hear words or see images but find it challenging to get the text on the page

- you've written and published but are searching for fresh inspiration

- you have ideas but don't know how or where to begin

- you feel the urge to write but have no ideas

- you're suffering with a bad case of writer's block

Whether you forge ahead organically or prefer to work with a detailed map, this book can help you become a more prolific and imaginative writer. If you do work with a map, you can use these techniques to go deep and write your outline. Later, you can use them to flesh it out. I've even included some plotting tools to get you started.

In Part 1, you'll learn about muses, meditation, visualization, and downshifting to create slower brain waves, a calm mind, and increased receptivity. I invite you to begin by listing your writing fears. But don't despair. Throughout the book, I've sprinkled several "Antidotes to Fear" that offer solutions for many of those blocks.

In Part 2, you'll write with your muse and learn writing and revising techniques. Each exercise is an invitation to "Try This." You can return to these visualizations whenever you like. Each session will be different. If you find it difficult to do this alone, watch my newsletter and website as I'll be inviting you to join me in guided visualizations online.

And in Parts 3 and 4, you'll apply what you've learned and go deeper.

My Story

I discovered this process unintentionally thirty years ago. At the time, I was going through a transition—leaving my marriage and starting a degree in Indigenous Studies. To cope with the stress, I started meditating. I remember lying flat out on a rug in corpse pose, sometimes for two or three hours. Soon, I experienced visions. Then characters appeared, and I began writing my first novel. I'd go to sleep and wake up with a scene playing in my mind. With my eyes closed, I'd watch until the end. Then, keeping in that relaxed state, I'd get up and type what I saw and heard. I completed the first draft of that novel and left it sealed in brown paper during many moves. Recently, I rewrote and published it as *Lure: Jesse & Hawk.* The first scene, where Jesse is photographing the deer, appeared in a dream exactly as I wrote it all those years ago.

I was unsure of my next step as commencement drew near. What does one do with a B.A. in Indigenous Studies? While returning home one day, I clearly heard someone say "rape crisis center." It was so real that I glanced over to the passenger seat. I heard it again. I'd never heard of a rape crisis center, and we drifted into an argument. When I arrived home, I found a voicemail from a friend who'd just joined the board of the Oshawa-Durham Rape Crisis Center. I trained there as a counselor, and that position evolved into a counseling role at a transition house, which ultimately led to a teaching position in British Columbia.

A guiding spirit? Perhaps. I've seen spirits from time to time. One Christmas Eve, I awoke to find someone standing at the foot of my bed. I was startled, but only felt love. On other occasions, usually during times of stress and transition, I've awakened feeling a presence in my room. I'd flip on the bedside light to find no one there. Guardian angels? Ancestors come to call? Perhaps. Those who love and watch out for us are never far away.

I've studied Druidry and Wicca, both of which offer a rich and fascinating world of psychic work. I've engaged in channeled writing and worked with stones and crystals, plants, animals, and sacred landscapes. I've traveled to walk in the footsteps of my characters, experienced the world through their eyes, and felt the impact of place on their soul and mine. I'm inspired by my muses and possess complete faith in them. I'm thrilled to have developed a strong bond with my hero and know he'll come when I call.

On the Ghost Trail

A few years ago, I decided to write a novel set at a lighthouse. I'd worked as a relief lighthouse keeper during 2013–2014 and lived at several stations on the British Columbia coast. Lighthouses are not only romantic; the spirits of people who've had their lives cut short frequently dwell there. I wanted to write a mystery about a young woman who returns to the historic lighthouse where she grew up. After experiencing serious trauma, her psychic abilities are triggered, and suddenly, like her mother and grandmother, she can commune with spirits.

I knew very little about spirits and those who saw them, so I started my research by reading books penned by famous mediums. Then my local metaphysical store advertised a mediumship class, and it passed across my screen just at the right moment. Has that ever happened to you? When those moments of synchronicity arise, it's wise to pay attention. I talked with Metta Joy[1], who was teaching the class, and decided to join.

We dove into the deep end the very first evening by engaging in Joy's meditation and then "reading" for each other. I wasn't surprised to discover I could see spirits with my inner eyes, and I'm no different than you. In fact, everyone in that class was able to engage in meditation and experience their psychic abilities. As we learned about clairvoyance, clairaudience, and clairsentience, things started to happen.

Genesis

During the mediumship session one afternoon, I saw a woman's hand emerge from the water, grasping a tree branch. She motioned for me to follow her. I reached out and grabbed the branch she offered, but her arm was long and thin, extending far into the water like a tentacle, and I didn't dare follow her down. That woman, as Joy put it,

---

1. https://joywisdom.ca/

might be one of my muses. I agreed with her, but couldn't help but think she was a reflection of myself.

The image reminded me of the scene at the end of *King Arthur* where the Lady of the Lake catches the sword, Excalibur. Such an archetype rang true for me, and I came home and journaled about creating a book called *From Spirit to Page: Writing with Your Muse.* I saw an image of a woman's arm rising from the water, but instead of a branch or sword, her hand was holding a quill. I felt energized and inspired. Something was afoot.

A friend channeled the spirit of my eighth-grade English teacher during a later session. I owe my early interest in writing to Mr. Sellers. He had confidence in me. He introduced me to the worlds of poetry, art, music, and bizarre foods like fried grasshoppers dipped in chocolate when I was growing up in rural Ontario. He took us country kids to see plays and concerts in Toronto.

On my eighteenth birthday, five years later, Mr. Sellers paid me a visit. I'd dropped out of school and moved into a squalid basement flat on Toronto's Balliol Street with a man serving time for smuggling cannabis. It was the 1970s, and I was a bit of a rebel at the time. Mr. Sellers showed up wearing a long fur coat. I still have the book he gave me, titled *I'm a Sensation*, which is full of drawings, photos, and rebel poetry. Since he didn't have much time left, he said, he wanted to have an impact on as many people as possible. I thought he might be ill. But a drunk driver struck and killed him on his way home from school six months later. Premonition? Perhaps. His passing devastated me for a long time.

When Mr. Sellers appeared in spirit at our session, the medium said, "I have a dark-haired man here. I feel like he's your teacher." Chills riveted through my body because I'd felt him too. Mr. Sellers stepped forward as she said, "He wants to talk to you."

We didn't launch into an animated conversation at that moment. Spirit doesn't work like that. But I felt different—more energized and alive—like a trusted friend walked beside me. And later, when I asked specific questions while in meditation, Mr. Sellers answered.

A few days after this session, I sat my laptop on the counter, opened a blank document, and started pacing. I'd walk away, walk back, and type something else. I wasn't thinking about what I was typing; I just let the words flow. In a couple of hours, I'd created the framework for four 2-hour workshops. It felt like pulling words from the wind and etching them on the page, and I'm certain that Mr. Sellers was there providing me with inspiration. I advertised, and five brave, curious women joined me. All of them wrote during those sessions and left wanting more time to explore writing with their muse. Their trust in me inspired confidence.

How do I know my experiences are real? Consciousness is a complex concept we'll tease out as we journey, so we'll return to this question along the way. But I'll start by saying this: My intuition led me to this moment and has guided me through writing several books. This process works for me and other writers like me, so I know that you too can write with your muse.

PART 1

MEETING YOUR MUSE

WHAT IS A MUSE?

"Tell me, O muse, of that ingenious hero who travelled far and wide after he had sacked the famous town of Troy." Homer, *The Odyssey*

The Classical Muse

The word muse derives from the Greek *mousa,* meaning a poet's inspiration or genius, and the concept springs from Classical Greek mythology. At Delphi and Sicyon lived the Three Muses, to whom a man could appeal for spiritual inspiration. Around 700–730 BCE, the Greek epic poet Hesiod created a tradition of the Nine Muses in *Theogony* that we accept today. Theogony refers to "the genealogy or birth of the gods," and his name, Hēsiodos, means *he who sends forth the voice.*[1]

These Nine Muses are the daughters of Zeus and the Titan, Mnemosyne, Goddess of Memory (mnemonics are memory devices). All are associated with artistic and creative

---

1. https://chs.harvard.edu/primary-source/hesiod-theo gony-sb/

endeavors. Calliope, for example, can influence a poet's ability to write epic poetry. The beloved Erato (think erotic) can help conjure love poetry, while Melpomene influences tragedy and Thalia, comedy.

A man—and in those days, authors were men—would appeal to a particular goddess for inspiration. And so, Homer begins his epic poem, *The Odyssey*, with an Invocation to the Goddess: "Tell me, O muse, of that ingenious hero who travelled far and wide after he had sacked the famous town of Troy."

The Odyssey, if we believe classicist and translator E. V. Rieu, was the first novel in Western Literature with its "well-knit plot, its psychological interest, and its interplay of characters" (Intro to the 1946 edition). [2]

Composed in Greek Ionia in the Eighth Century BCE, *The Odyssey* could well be considered the first epic fantasy novel with its monsters, gods, and supernatural villains who thwart the hero, Odysseus, on his ten-year journey home from the Trojan War. The tale certainly follows the mythological structure of "The Hero's Journey," something we'll delve into in more detail in a later chapter.

As a child, I was obsessed with mythological movies. *Ulysses* (1954) and *Jason and the Argonauts* (1963) were two films I watched repeatedly on Sunday afternoons. I was steeped in "The Hero's Journey" long before I discovered comparative

---

2. Homer. The Odyssey. E.V. Rieu translator, Introduction by Peter Jones. Penguin Classics: London, 2003

mythologist Joseph Campbell and *The Power of Myth* in my thirties.[3]

It's important to note that the classical relationship between man and muse originally occurred on a spiritual level, because later, after the advent of traditional religion, Goddess worship was derailed and the notion of the muse changed.

The Changing Muse

Later, a mortal woman, usually an individual the author adored and held in high esteem, became a poet's muse. He may have lusted after her. He may have been romantically involved with her. He may have been obsessed with her. And though his love was often unrequited, his passion drove him to create with and for his muse, the source of his inspiration.

Italian poet Dante's muse Beatrice served as an inspiration in the twelfth century, and two centuries later, Petrarch wrote love sonnets with the lady Laura in mind. In this same fashion, the Romantic poets often chose a beautiful woman as their muse. And in the nineteenth century, W.B. Yeats, who was mad for Maud Gonne, wrote countless poems to conjure her love, which, sadly, he never attained. He then turned his attention to her daughter, Iseult, and she became his muse. Unfortunately, when he proposed, daughter, like mother, refused him.

---

3. Campbell, Joseph with Bill Moyers. The Power of Myth. Betty Sue Flowers, editor. Doubleday: NY, 1988.

The Contemporary Muse

Fortunately, times have changed again. Men are no longer the only published authors, and women are no longer the only muses. At a time when anyone and everyone can write and publish, the muse can take as many shapes as the medium.

Comparative mythologist Joseph Campbell has been one of my muses for thirty years. His wisdom has guided me through life, and his teachings on the "Hero's Journey" are ingrained in my psyche. Among the gold nuggets he offers is this: When you're caught by an author, songwriter, or poet, explore everything you can created by them.

Another of my muses is singer-songwriter Peter Gabriel, and I'm experiencing his music in a whole new way as I dive into the sound and meaning of his songs. Peter Gabriel's voice inspired Conall Ceol, one of my favorite characters in *To Kill a King* and *To Dance with Destiny*. Conall is a sensitive warrior and gifted Druid bard from Iron Age Ireland. This is Estrada's reaction when he first hears him sing:

One August, Estrada had come upon a six-hundred-year-old yellow cedar tree that had been split by lightning only moments before. Its flesh was shredded in long furls, and its raw, smoky perfume caught in his throat and brought tears to his eyes. Electricity shook the leaves like a shaman's rattle. Somewhere between smoke and brandied sap, its sticky blood drizzled down the rasps. He folded forward into its golden smoke. He thought of it now as he listened to Conall's voice. It caught his gut like an iron fist and

drew him in. Leaning over, he closed his eyes. He wanted more. He wanted to curl into Conall's yellow cedar soul and steam. — *To Kill a King*

In essence, artists who were once inspired by the muses themselves can become *your* muse. This is how literature continues to flow through generations. Words, beats, and images transcend time and space in this ongoing conversation.

So, if your feet are stuck in the sand, pull them out and dive into the pool where others have swum before. Soak up the inspiration of your creative mentors.

In writing this book, I find myself traveling back to the words of my own muses. You'll find them sprinkled throughout this book, in quotes, in wisdom, and in words. Now, like never before, you have at your fingertips a vast array of inspiration. In releasing and allowing these voices to resonate, you'll embark on a journey Ulysses would have adored.

I propose that there is not just one muse for every artist but several who wear many guises—the muse within and the muse without. Regardless of gender, culture, or religion, the muse awaits and need only be invoked. This book will help you find and write with your muse.

A Muse With Many Faces

"I am convinced that all poetry is, as Emerson said, first written in the heavens, that is, it is conceived by a self deeper than appears in normal life, and when it speaks to us its ancient story we taste of eternity and drink the soma juice, the elixir of immortality." Æ, pseudonym for Irish poet, artist, and mystic, George William Russell

The Muse Within

Some people believe that all intuitive knowledge, in whatever form, comes from a divine source. Call it God. Call it Universal Energy. Call it The Great Mystery. Call it The Force. Whatever you believe is personal and doesn't affect your ability to connect with your muse. Whether you believe in a muse within (your divine soul or higher self) or without (another entity that connects with you) doesn't matter either. What matters is knowing you have the power to access creative inspiration.

I personally believe there is a force within my soul that will communicate with me if I'm in danger or ask for guidance. This is my intuitive voice and sense of inner knowing, something I call The Muse Within.

The Muse Without

I also believe in spiritual energy, which includes characters who become real, spirit guides, angels, and people who've passed on. I refer to these beings as The Muse Without.

Characters Who Become Real

Estrada, who is the hero of the Hollystone Mysteries, first came to me in 2006. I didn't make him up. One day, he just appeared. Estrada is a polyamorous, bisexual magician who works at a Goth club in Vancouver. But if you ask him, he'll tell you that the most important thing in his life is his position as High Priest for Hollystone, a coven of Vancouver witches.

I've chronicled Estrada's adventures for years, and he's always been easy to write, though he's a very different personality type than I am. Estrada is an extroverted, sensation-seeking showman who falls in love hard and fast, usually with the wrong people. He's flawed and often makes bad decisions, but he'll do anything to save those he loves. Like many of the characters in this series, I fell in love with him. Then, like Margery Williams' *Velveteen Rabbit*, he became real.

At one of my strangest mediumship sessions, the woman who was reading for me talked of a man who was a dark, handsome adventurer—a kind of sexy swashbuckler who was up for anything. He was no one I knew in this lifetime and sounded way too much like Estrada to be anyone else.

She can't be talking about my character, I thought. *That's just too weird.* But even as I thought it, I felt the riveting goosebumps of truth.

The teacher asked, "How does Wendy know him?"

My reader paused a moment and said, "I feel like he's not a real person, like maybe she created him?" *Whoa.* More goosebumps.

Characters can become real. And when they do, writers are the luckiest people on Earth.

We become richer, bolder, and more authentic with our muse by our side. Plus, you can conjure your character whenever you're ready to write the next book in your series.

Spirit Guides

Over the years, I've become aware of several of my personal spirit guides. In my early thirties, I was torn between Indigenous Studies, which fed my soul, and English Literature, which intrigued me. I went to see a psychic in Ontario, who clearly saw two spirits standing behind me. One was an Indigenous man from a past life who I'd seen before in a vision, and the other was a strong female poet who resembled Emily Dickinson. Both spirits were vying to win me over to their wishes, and the result was confusion and indecision. I was stuck.

The psychic told me to tell them to back off and let me make my own choice, which is the best advice she could have given me. And so I share it here with you. Please remember that you are not at the mercy of your spirit guides. They should support you, not coerce or pressure you. If ever you feel you aren't in charge of your life, or someone is telling you to do something questionable, something you're not ready to do, or something you're uncomfortable with, please seek professional help. *If it's not absolutely yes, it's positively no.*

At the time, I went with my heart and chose Indigenous Studies. During the course of my learning, my seventy-five-year-old mother revealed that her father's family was Dutch and Tuscarora (the Sixth Nation of the Iroquois Confederacy). Whether that influenced my lifelong obsession with Indigenous Studies, I can't say. But I wonder if I'd gone another route—would my mother have ever mentioned this ancestor at all? Sometimes I feel my great-great grandmother's presence. She wants me to write her story, which I intend to do. Regardless, the healing I received while studying with traditional Elders and teachers in Ontario affected me in profound ways.

When I moved to British Columbia and applied to the teaching program, I was told that a degree in Indigenous Studies was wonderful, but it wasn't a teachable subject. I'd need something else to qualify for the Professional Development Program. I hope times have changed. I ended up completing a Diploma in English Literature before I went into teaching. I taught English for many years and worked as the Aboriginal Education Coordinator in one district. So, both spirit guides eventually got their wish.

Angels

I'm not proficient in angel work, though I call in my angels from time to time and ask for help. There are some amazing people teaching how to work with angels. My favorite angel expert is Kyle Gray.[1]

I often call my angels and spirit guides together to assist me. "Angels and Spirit Guides, please help me shut down the chatter in my brain. I need to sleep now." As simple as it sounds, this works.

Supportive Spirits from Your Past

In the introduction, I wrote about how the spirit of Mr. Sellers appeared at a mediumship session, wanting to talk to me. During my nightly meditation, when I asked him about spirits, he showed me a galaxy of stars. Each star was the spirit of someone who'd passed. The spirits of those who've left aren't living in some gated community in the clouds. Their loving energy is all around us, and they're here to help. This starry vision of life after death is something Estrada experiences after his ordeal in *To Render a Raven*.

At mediumship sessions that year, several of my deceased uncles came through to me and to others reading for me. One man seemed very much like one of my uncles, but I didn't think it could be him because he was still alive. Then I Googled him and discovered his obituary. Uncle Bud just wanted me to know he missed me and was still

---

1. https://www.kylegray.co.uk

looking out for me. That gave me comfort, as he'd worked for many years as a Deputy Police Chief in Welland, Ontario. In his later years, he helped me research my father's family history, and that's how we bonded.

None of the spirits that appeared brought anything negative. They all came with love and offered supportive messages. If you're receiving negative messages or being told to do something hurtful, shut down and get assistance. Spirits are only here to support and inspire us on our journey.

In mediumship, we learned how to blend with spirits so we could communicate. Once we leave this body, our spirit vibrates at a much higher rate than it does in our dense body. To blend and connect, spirits must slow down their vibration while we raise ours. When we're open, we meet at the edges of our aura, which is an energy field that extends a few feet out from our physical body.

Spirits often communicate in symbols that are personally meaningful to each of us. When I do readings, a star is the symbol for spirit, which may be why Mr. Sellers showed me stars funneling down around me. Each of us has different symbols because we're all unique and develop our own language with which to connect and interpret spirit.

When I opened my mind to the study of mediumship and psychic development, my writing blossomed. Now, I can't stop the flow of words and ideas.

Other Creative Souls

This includes people, both alive and dead, who influence and inspire us. There's a reason we're drawn to certain authors, songwriters, musicians, artists, and poets. Works resound in the Collective Unconscious. Archetypes, symbols, stories, and myths are universal. Don't believe me? How many renditions of Cinderella or Little Red Riding Hood appear in cultures around the world? Evil threatens good every day, everywhere.

Like Mr. Sellers, your job as a writer is to touch people's lives. Is that too grand a task? Are you, like the reluctant hero, wanting to turn back now?

Every time you light a candle in the darkness to conjure hope, every time your hero beats down the villain, every time the killer is caught and justice is served, you've done your job. Through every poem that utters beauty and truth, through every true story you share, through every smile and every tear you conjure, you've used your gift in a positive way.

A Word of Warning

Remember that you're always in charge. You establish the boundaries. You do the asking, and when you ask a question, you'll get an answer, though it may not be the answer you expected. So, please be mindful of your thoughts and careful what you ask for.

When I was writing *To Kill a King*, a Druid warrior whacked one of my main characters on the top of the head with the flat edge of an Iron Age sword. Although I saw it happen, I didn't feel it. And since this had never happened to me, I sat at my laptop, wondering. *What would it feel like? Would it knock Sorcha unconscious? Daze her? How painful would a blow like that be? Would she bleed? Could it kill her?*

The next morning, I pulled into the Costco parking lot and opened my hatchback. I'd been driving this vehicle for ten years, and this had never happened before. I swear. I stood behind the car, took out my cloth bag, and slammed the trunk down on the top of my head! Metal to skull. *Clang.* The first thought that flashed through my mind was: *Sorcha! This is how it felt. Only ten times worse.*

Fortunately, my muse only gave me a taste. I didn't pass out, though I was momentarily stunned. I shook it off and stumbled into Costco, where I asked the woman checking cards to please check my skull. There was a red mark, but no blood. I pushed the cart around the store, mostly to regain my equilibrium so I could drive. I couldn't touch that spot for days. So, please be careful what you ask for.

TRY THIS: DISPELLING FEAR

"Tools are totems, an important weapon in the fight against fear." Ralph Keyes, *The Courage to Write*

Intro

Your muse is ready to inspire you, just waiting for you to begin your writing journey. All of us carry personal fears, so before you start, it's a good idea to reflect on what might be holding you back.

The word *dispel* seems appropriate because of its association with the word, *spell*. A spell is an incantation used as a magical charm. As you might know, spells create powerful thought forms. A spell can be spoken or written, ripple into the ether to affect others, and have lasting effects. Often, we invoke fear spells on ourselves or others without knowing it. But spells can be broken, and to dispel a spell is to break it so that its power shatters and it can no longer control you.

You're about to generate a list of personal fears about writing. Don't fret. I've experienced and explored many fears myself over the years and continue to write, now more than ever. I've also talked to many writers about their fears and coping skills. I've sprinkled "Antidotes to Fear" throughout this book that I hope will help you find your way through fear and into writing.

Objectives:

- Become aware of blocks

- Free yourself to access your muse

- Begin to heal your writing life

Tools:

If you don't already have a blank journal, you'll need to purchase one. The only criteria is that you're drawn to it and use it regularly. If you like tangibles, go with pen and paper. If you prefer typing, you can create a writing journal on your laptop, phone, or iPad. I like to type, but if I work on my laptop at night in bed, it keeps me awake for hours, so my preference is low light in the evening, perhaps even candlelight, a pen, and a journal.

If you have any meditation tracks (music only), you might listen to one before you begin or as you work.

Sequence:

Read this sequence first, so you know what's coming.

Open your journal and have your pen at hand. Either sit cross-legged or in a chair with your feet flat on the floor and back straight. Close your eyes and take a few deep breaths, in through your nose and out through pursed lips. Then just breathe normally and bring your awareness to the air flowing in and out of your nostrils. Feel the muscles in your body relax, especially your shoulders, neck, and jaw. If thoughts intrude, notice and let them go. Don't rush. Give yourself time to clear your mind.

When you feel ready, write the title "MY WRITING FEARS" at the top of the page. Then write whatever comes to mind. One fear may feed off another. This includes everything to do with writing—the actual writing process, what to do with your finished writing, how your writing might be received, or how becoming a writer might change your life. Some of these things will no doubt reach back into your early years, to a time of genesis with deep psychological underpinnings. Stories and images may emerge. Jot it all down.

Don't be afraid. You might recall an awkward or embarrassing moment, an incident that angered or terrified you, or a time when you felt humiliated or heartbroken.

One way to break a spell is to expose it. Light is always an antidote to darkness, and fears, like secrets, thrive in the dark. The longer you keep them hidden, the stronger they become. But Freedom is the antidote to Fear.

You may feel vulnerable. But know this: The other way to break a fear spell is through trust. Trust yourself and your innate, intuitive muse.

Now, open your journal, find a comfortable position and begin to breathe. When you feel ready, write.

When it feels complete, read it. Are you surprised by anything you've written? Did something come up that you'd like to explore further? Is there something in these words that could be holding you back?

Afterward, you may delete the list, burn it in a special ritual, smudge it with sage, or frame it and hang it on your wall. Trust that you'll know what to do.

Common Writing Beliefs & Fears

Do you see any of your fears in this list? Some are my own personal fears. Others I've heard from other writers.

I can't write. I was a terrible writer in school. My essays came back covered in red circles and with bad grades. I'll always be a terrible writer.

I don't have time. I get ideas, but I'm too busy to write them down in any kind of form.

Scenes swirl in my head, but I can't get the words on the page.

No one will want to read anything I write. No one will like my blog post or buy *my* book.

I can only write when I'm sad, angry, or emotional. When life is good, I have nothing to say and no inspiration at all.

If my mother reads what I write, she'll be embarrassed, appalled, or ashamed.

There are millions of ebooks, and bookstore shelves are crammed. No one will ever choose my book.

People will judge me. I'll be criticized, ridiculed, and slammed on social media.

People will look at me differently.

Writing something down on paper gives it power. It could come back to haunt me. I might get sued.

I'm dyslexic. I have lots of ideas, but I fear I can't get them on paper properly.

No agent or publisher will ever accept my writing. I can't stand rejection.

The last book I queried was rejected every time. I must be a terrible writer. Why bother?

If I'm successful, I'll have to climb out of my cave and sell myself. I'm way too introverted and afraid to speak in public.

I could self-publish, but I'll never learn it all.

I don't know how or where to start.

FREEDOM is the opposite of FEAR. As you acknowledge your fears, you begin to dissolve the blocks and forge a free space from which to write. Try writing your own acronym.

False Evidence Appearing Real
Finding Excuses and Reasons
Freedom Ends Active Resistance
F*ck Everything and Rise

Antidote to Fear: Writing Woes

I can't write. I was a terrible writer in school. My essays came back covered in red circles and streaks and bad grades. I'll always be a terrible writer.

I taught literature and creative writing for almost twenty-five years to secondary students and am guilty of using the red pen. I can tell you that my intention was to help by pointing out places needing revision, though I'm sure I instilled this fear in some of my students. Most of us experienced teachers who damaged our psyches in some way. I dropped out of high school in grade 11, believing I could write but that I'd never learn science or math because I'd failed both subjects.

Leaping from "I was a terrible writer in school" to "I'll *always* be a terrible writer" is a limiting assumption. Connecting with your muse will help you get your ideas onto the page. Once there, that draft must be revised and edited. You can join critique groups, hire an editor, engage beta readers, or use an online spelling and grammar checker. Now that we have the Internet, you don't need to know everything. Experiment, and choose the tools that work for you. These days, you can even ask AI to sweeten your writing.

Sylvia Ashton-Warner[1] taught Maori children in New Zealand using something she called "Key Vocabulary." She wrote about how words have intense meaning and are based on life experience. Key vocabulary centers around two main instincts—fear and sex—and varies depending on culture and location. Young readers have a private key vocabulary that the teacher can discover through talking with them. Ashton-Warner allowed the children to choose their own words—those with intense personal meaning. She would write one word on a card, have the child trace the letters and spell it out loud, then teach the word to another child. As the children collected words, they formed a creative autobiographical story and illustrated it. The stories were kept private and confidential, and the content wasn't judged or criticized. This is memoir at its rawest and most potent.

Sylvia supported the children by asking guiding questions and recording their personal lists of words in the backs of their notebooks. In this way, the child became both a writer and a reader. Each day, new words were revealed based on life experience, thoughts, feelings, and the need to know. Sometimes, the children read each other's books and made connections.

---

1. Ashton-Warner, Sylvia. Teacher. Simon & Schuster: New York, 1963.

Writing is intensely personal, as Sylvia Ashton-Warner points out, and if we aren't judged but rather supported in our explorations of words and their meaning, we're all writers. It begins one word at a time, with personally meaningful context.

MEDITATION & VISUALIZATION

"Writing is a spiritual practice in that people that have no spiritual path can undertake it and, as they write, they begin to wake up to a larger connection. After a while, people tend to find that there is some muse that they are connecting to." Julia Cameron[1]

A few years ago, I took a course in Buddhism through Simon Fraser University in British Columbia. The Zen monk who taught us led excursions to several Buddhist temples in the Lower Mainland. On one of these visits, I remember a monk saying something like this: I don't understand why people travel. We can go anywhere in our mind, just by closing our eyes and following our breath.

He was referring to his experiences using meditation and visualization. Personally, I like to physically travel to the locations where I set my stories. The energy of the landscape, plus the physical and sensory experience, allows

---

1. https://juliacameronlive.com/

me to connect with my characters on another level, and I discover little details that take my readers inside. See my chapter on "Living Research" for more on that. I do, however, use this process to work with my muse in the creative phase.

Meditation is often associated with Buddhism or yoga, but it doesn't have to be. All five major religions use a form of meditation: Hinduism, Buddhism, Judaism, Christianity, and Islam. But you don't need religion to meditate. It's a tool that allows you to close down the chatter of "monkey mind" (the restless, confused, unsettled mind) and lower the frequencies of your brainwaves. See "The Science of Spirit" for more information.

Mentors

Natalie Goldberg[2] is a poet, memoirist, Zen Buddhist practitioner, and writing teacher. Her book, *Writing Down the Bones* (1986), is a classic on free-writing that I recommend. If it's not in your local library, check used book stores. Goldberg now leads weeklong, silent retreats where participants spend twenty minutes in sitting meditation, twenty minutes in walking meditation, and twenty minutes writing. Then they read their musings aloud.

Julia Cameron followed up with *The Artist's Way* in 1992. Writing "morning pages" is now something many people

---

2. Goldberg, Natalie. The True Secret of Writing: Connecting Life with Language. Atria: New York, 2013

do, not just to write and unleash blocks but to heal. Since then, Cameron has furthered her work with new books, and now offers an online video course.

Actress Goldie Hawn brought MindUP[3] to children and teachers years ago. I completed the training and used the techniques at the beginning of my high school English classes to bring us all together in a calm, focused way. I was delighted with the kids' responses. If I skipped our practice and plunged right into the lesson, they stopped me and requested it. Sometimes, we just closed our eyes and watched our breath. Most times, I took them on a journey, and that they liked best.

There are several types of meditation, but all agree that the practice promotes health and wellbeing by lowering stress and increasing creativity. Why wouldn't you meditate? Here are a few variations that I've tried over the years. Why not explore them and see what works best for you?

Mindfulness Meditation

Start by turning off all distractions. Sit or lie in a relaxed position and follow your breath in and out. It may help to repeat *inhale/exhale* in your mind or watch your chest expand and contract. One Buddhist monk told us to imagine a tiny pea sitting at the edge of a nostril. When thoughts come, and they will, don't judge. Just notice and let them go. The idea is to calm the mind by becoming

---

3. https://mindup.org/

aware of the flurry of thoughts that distract us in each moment. The goal is to be present and aware.

Mindfulness is one of the most challenging meditations because the mind loves to spin. But there is no right or wrong.

I decide to sit and practice mindfulness meditation for twenty minutes four times a week. Twenty minutes isn't long, I tell myself, unless you're on a long-haul bus in Ireland and you really have to pee, you're starving, or you're waiting for someone to come, or go. I press the timer on my phone, close my eyes, and begin. I hear a finch outside, the dogs sniffing at the door, my daughter's cough, footsteps on the stairs (*probably dogs.*) I notice I'm sitting forward, breathing shallow and fast. I sit back and watch my breath. Imagine a string holding up my marionette head. I hear a buzzy fly. My son-in-law sings a note and my grandson sings it back. *Maybe I didn't start the timer. Twenty minutes must have passed by now.* I resist the urge to open my eyes and push the button. *Breathe in. Breathe out. Maybe I should just check. 1:24 left to go. Hah.* This is what mindfulness meditation can be like. Try again, tomorrow. —Wendy's Journal, June 22, 2023

Movement Meditation

Have you ever joined someone on a nature walk, hoping to relax and take in everything around you, then found your partner talked the entire time? Or maybe you were the one talking—on your cell phone or to your friend? In movement meditation, the idea is not to talk, or even think, but to experience by noticing details like the way the muscles in your foot connect with the sand. Some Buddhist programs combine sitting meditation with walking meditation over a period of time. After sitting for twenty minutes, a gong sounds, and everyone quietly gets up and walks for twenty minutes. Then they come back to sit.

My characters often chat with me or with each other when I'm walking in the woods. I love this because I'm actively listening to them. Often, I'll turn on my audio app and record what they say. Nature walks are one of the best ways to move and meditate, but also be aware of what's happening in your mind when you're gardening, practicing yoga or tai chi, cleaning, or floating on your back in water. These, too, can be openings for your muse.

Visualization

This is one of my favorite types of meditation. The idea is to quiet the mind and then imagine yourself in a particular place. As you meander, notice the sensory details. What do you see, hear, smell, taste, and feel?

There are hundreds of visualizations online. One of my favorite sources is The Honest Guys[4] on Youtube. If you're a Tolkien fan, try their "Middle Earth Meditations."

Druid psychologist and psychotherapist, Philip Carr-Gomm [5] has been leading comforting visualizations

---

4. https://www.youtube.com/@TheHonestGuys/videos

5. https://philipcarr-gomm.com/

where Druid practitioners from all over the world meet together in a virtual oak grove for years. His weekly online "Tea with a Druid" show is live from Britain on Mondays at 8pm. Someone compiled all the meditations, and you can access them on YouTube.[6]

In Druidry, Awen (pronounced ah-oo-enn) is a Welsh word meaning *magical force that brings inspiration and illumination*. I think of Awen as being akin to the Muse. Druids often intone it three times, either alone or in ceremony, silently or in a deep, resonating voice. Inspiration is essential to bards who are the storytellers, musicians, and artists, of the Druid tradition, so experiencing Awen is their goal.

---

6. https://zodogo.com/yewtube/

THE SCIENCE OF SPIRIT

"Doubt, depression, pessimistic thoughts, lack of will, weaken the flow of healing life energies; the conscious direction of the mind's powers by positive thoughts, prayers, affirmations, visualization, will, cheerfulness, stimulates the natural healing processes of the body with the vital life force necessary to aid in restoring health." Paramahansa Yogananda

Once dismissed as new-age nonsense, scientists now expound on the power of visualization. I remember how, in the tragic years after AIDS surfaced, some patients visualized cancer cells as enemy troops and successfully bombed them. Now, it's been proven that stroke victims who visualize moving a paralyzed limb can save the tissue because the brain will send blood to the area whether it physically moves or not. Athletes, artists, CEOs, people ill or injured, and anyone wanting to gain focus and relief from stress can use this technique with positive results. How does it work?

Research reveals that whether you perform an action or imagine that action, the same regions in the brain are stimulated. Like fans of *Instagram*, the brain craves images and responds to them. This complex organ releases the appropriate chemicals (cortisol, endorphins, and dopamine) whether you're reading a story, creating a story, or, I'll take it one step further, receiving messages from spirit.

The occipital lobe, located at the back of the head, manages vision and imagination. It's engaged when we're reading and imagining, and when we're visualizing our scenes as writers. The frontal lobe (forehead—Third Eye Chakra) is the area of higher-level thinking. The temporal lobes, above our ears, hold memory; while the amygdala, dead center, is the home of our emotions. So, when we're visualizing a scene or receiving a scene from spirit and writing those words on the page, our brains are as dazzling as a starry night sky in the country.

Can you see that? Have you ever had a vivid dream or meditation with emotions more intense than anything you've ever experienced in your ordinary reality? That's because it's pure and raw, with no distractions or barriers.

Writers are luminaries. What we envision is taken into our reader's or listener's brain and stimulates a private pyrotechnic show. That, dear writer, is a reason to continue.

Whether you find it easy or difficult to close your eyes and see images within the darkened theater of your mind, the more often you practice, the better you'll become. I used to visualize frequently, but then I got caught up in the work-a-day world. As my stress levels soared, my ability to "see" diminished. So I began again. I put in my headphones, closed my eyes and journeyed with The Honest Guys[1] on YouTube. Once I began a regular practice, images appeared.

Visualization is one type of meditation, and, like all forms of meditation, there is a sequence you can follow to signal to your brain of the intention to slow down and focus on your inner world.

Meditation Tips

WEAR COMFORTABLE CLOTHING THAT WILL KEEP YOU WARM. There's nothing like cold feet to distract you and ruin a beautiful session.

FIND A QUIET PLACE where you can sit or lie down comfortably and not be disturbed.

GATHER YOUR WRITING TOOLS AND PLACE THEM BESIDE YOU.

PRE-READ THE SEQUENCE AND PERHAPS RECORD IT AS AN AUDIO FILE. I often do that so I can *listen* rather than think about what's coming next. Remember, the goal is to stop thinking and start connecting.

SILENCE TECHNOLOGY.

CONSIDER SETTING A TIMER.

CHOOSE A COMFORTABLE, RESTFUL POSITION. Some people sit in the traditional cross-legged pose you might be familiar with from yoga. Others prefer a straight-backed chair

---

1. https://www.youtube.com/@TheHonestGuys/playlists

where they can place their feet flat on the floor and connect with the Earth. Still others, like myself, prefer to lie flat and not think at all about the body. The only caution with this is, you might fall asleep. If you do, it's probably because you need sleep, so don't fret about it. Just come back and try again. (I sometimes wake up with a snort!) You might experiment by trying a different position for each practice. The idea is to free up restrictions so energy can travel through the physical and spiritual bodies.

EXPERIMENT WITH RITUALS. You might darken the room, add calming music, and light a candle or incense to change the energy and signal your mind that it's time.

ALWAYS COME BACK FULLY INTO YOUR BODY AND GROUND YOURSELF after you've engaged in a spiritual practice. Take a few deep breaths. Visualize the soles of your feet connected to the Earth. You might imagine roots spreading through layers of rock and sediment. Rub your hands together. Touch your face and rub your palms over the top of your head. Imagine a shield spread over the outside of your body.

BRAIN WAVES

"If we can consciously tap into the autonomic nervous system, we can begin to influence the way our body functions physiologically." Dr. Joe Dispenza

Some people may consider this a load of *malarkey* (a good old Irish word I learned from my father). So, let me explain how science and spirit intertwine to support you in co-creating.

Within each of our brains are masses of neurons that communicate with each other. The electrical impulses they create produce brainwaves that can be detected using sensors. Each vibrates at a particular bandwidth and can be associated with specific emotions and behaviors. Slow, low-frequency brainwaves create sleepy, dreamy states, whereas higher frequencies make us feel hyper, tense, anxious, and wired. Brainwave speed is measured in Hertz (cycles per second).

Beta Waves—14-24 Hz

The brain is awake, alert, conscious, focused externally, and using five senses to try to make sense of the external world.

This is a highly left-brained state of thinking, judging, and problem-solving. When we're scanning social media, arranging, organizing, working on finances and promotion schemes, doing our taxes or certain types of research, studying, learning, and taking tests, we're in a beta state. The problem is that over-activating and over-working beta leads to anxiety, stress, exhaustion, and tension. It's the chaotic, jumpy "monkey mind" we want to tame. This is also the place of fear, depression, and shattered confidence that reveal a disconnection from Source.

Dr. Joe Dispenza explains three levels of beta brainwaves that stretch from sensory awareness to hyper-arousal, where we're focused on survival and expressing emotions such as anger, anxiety, and pain. You can learn more on his website "Unlimited" at https://drjoedispenza.com.

For a certain amount of time, as writers, we must experience the beta state. Intense research, editing, writing academic papers, financial work, marketing, and day-to-day activities keep us mired there. But this is not the place to meet your muse. If you're sitting staring at the computer in a beta state, you'll undoubtedly experience writer's block because you're thinking too much and your brain is flooded with beta waves. Release the dam and let your imagination flow.

Alpha Waves—8-13 Hz

The brain is alert and lucid but in a state of relaxed thought. This is when we're daydreaming, lightly meditating, visualizing, tuned into spirit, and working creatively. We're feeling more balanced, happier, and enjoying increased serotonin levels. Here, you're receptive to meeting your muse. You might focus on research, revisions, marketing schemes, correspondence, and presentations. You might also try channeled writing here.

Theta Waves—4-7.5 Hz

Theta is my favorite place. It's a deeply relaxed, balanced state where we experience deep meditation, subconscious creativity, vivid visual imagery, creative inspiration, and flowing ideas and connections. This is where we fully connect with our muses. It often occurs in the twilight time between waking and sleeping. Here, your right brain is engaged. You know you're in the zone, a place of intuition, creativity, and vision. It's the realm of the muse, and you can get there through meditation.

Delta Waves—0.5-4 Hz

Delta is the state of enlightened meditation, physical rejuvenation and healing, expanded awareness, intuition, and insight that we experience in deep dreamless sleep and unconscious states. These low, slow brainwaves are like a drumbeat or heartbeat, either our own or that of Mother Earth.

TRY THIS: AWARENESS

It can be fascinating and helpful to develop personal awareness by reflecting on your daily states of mind. The only stipulation is to be honest with yourself.

Throughout this book, I'll offer activities and suggestions to increase alpha and theta activity.

Objective:

- To become more aware of your states of mind, how they shift, and how you can consciously shift them

Tools:

- Journal and pen, or laptop

Sequence:

Open your journal and have your pen at hand. Either sit cross-legged or in a chair with your feet flat on the floor and back straight. Close your eyes and take a few deep breaths, in through your nose and out through pursed lips. Then just breathe normally and bring your awareness to the air flowing in and out of your nostrils. Feel the muscles in your body relax—your shoulders, neck, and jaw. If thoughts intrude, notice and let them go. Don't rush. Give yourself time to clear your mind.

When you feel ready, open your eyes. Read and reflect on each question that follows and jot down anything that comes to you.

How much time do I spend with a rollicking "monkey mind" and/or working on analytical activities that keep me tied to the beta state (business, marketing, engaging with social media)? Does my career or current job keep me mired in beta brain?

Does my intuition try to reach me to help me shift from beta to alpha? Perhaps by giving me a headache or tense muscles? Do I listen or ignore the call?

How do I shift from a beta state to a creative state (alpha and theta)?

If I awaken in the morning with words or images in my mind, do I take the time to record everything I can remember?

When I'm drafting, do I get into a creative space and then shift back into beta because I feel the need to edit right away? Could I just write and leave edits and revisions until later?

Could I set up a specific time to just breathe and write without thinking or stopping?

What triggers me to shift my brainwaves? Perhaps a walk in the woods or time by the ocean? A candlelight bath? A yoga session? Deep breathing? Ten minutes of meditation in a quiet place?

Can I make an agreement with myself to spend more time in the alpha and theta states?

As you reflect, stories and images may emerge. Capture it all on your page. Becoming aware is the first step in making changes.

TRY THIS: MEET YOUR MUSE

"All the arts depend upon telepathy to some degree, but I believe that writing offers the purest distillation." Stephen King, *On Writing: A Memoir of the Craft*[1]

Objectives:

- experience visualization

- meet your muse

Tools:

- Journal and pen, or laptop

Sequence:

When you feel ready to meet your muse, relax in whatever position feels most natural to you. Begin by drawing your awareness to your breath, either to your rising belly or the edges of your nostrils. Breathe in cool air and breathe out warm air. *Breathe in. Breathe out.* Feel your muscles relax. Scan your body slowly from toes to crown, simply becoming aware of any places where you might be holding tension. Pay particular attention to your shoulders, neck, jaw, and tongue. If you encounter tension, breathe it out until you feel a sense of release, then move on. Continue to follow your breath in and out, and as you do, simply *breathe in, breathe out.*

Your body begins to feel heavier and sinks like sediment to the bottom of a pool. As your spirit clears and lifts, a soft glow forms around you. *Breathe in. Breathe out.* Now, draw your awareness to the space in your forehead directly between your eyebrows and about an inch above. This is the Third Eye, the root of the pineal gland, and the theater of visualization.

Here you can draw back a pair of velvety curtains to reveal images, words, colors, and sensations.

Tonight's play is called "The Muse." You can see the title written in fiery bronze letters on a sign center stage. The play is set almost three thousand years ago in Ancient

Greece, where Homer is writing *The Odyssey* and the first festival of the Olympic Games is beginning its historic four-year cycle. You stare at the fiery bronze letters and wait, for you know "The Muse" is about to appear.

On either side of the sign is a large pottery urn with twin handles. Light illuminates the painted rings of black geometric markings circling its sides. There are triangles, lightning bolts, horses, and chariots. You have a sense that the vase was intended for some purpose, and you wonder what it could be. Perhaps the answer comes to you as you examine the markings.

As the light fades and the stage darkens, the vase disappears and a new figure emerges. It's a woman. A goddess. Take your time and just be with her. Observe. Listen. Sense. And remember.

Without thinking, pick up your pen and freely write words and phrases as they come. Don't read them. Don't judge them. Just write them. And don't stop writing until the words stop flowing. You'll know when it's time. Then ground yourself with a couple of deep breaths and open your eyes.

Revise:

Read aloud what you wrote. How does it make you feel? Surprised? Intrigued? Your words may have nothing to do with the goddess. Don't judge, just go with it. If you're completely new to meditation or in a distracted state, you may need to try again at another time. But do come back to it and record the words you receive through your muse.

At this point, you can make changes. Add, delete, or shift things around. You've made the connection with the muse, and the words are on the page. Now, make it yours.

My Example:

Below is the first draft of what I wrote. Note that it's not just images of what I see while meditating. The beginnings of a poem are here in the phrases.

Azure eyes flashing like an Aegean Sea
The ships have left the harbor
Caught in the winds of change, their sails billow
Men scamper up masts and rigging,
Tanned skin glowing in the morning sun
Her bronze sandals lace up sturdy legs
Strong runner, huntress.
In her hand she hefts a bow,
White dress billowing like the sails as she follows on the winds
Breathing heart into intrepid travelers searching for home

When I revise, I move into an alpha state. Rather than just describe, I add action and emotion to create the beginnings of a storyline. Notice that my poem has taken the shape of a pottery urn or perhaps a woman. The white space around words and the shape of the words on the page create form and are another aspect of writing.

Goddess

Azure eyes flashing like the Aegean Sea
She watches as the ship leaves safe harbor
Caught in the winds of war, sails billowing.
Rugged men scamper up masts and rigging,
Tanned skin glowing like the morning sun.
Her bronze sandals lace up sturdy legs.
Strong runner. Goddess. Huntress.
In her hand she hefts a bow,
Arrow nocked and ready.
When a blood drop hits her cheek, she frets for them.
Pale gown unfurling, she rises, circling in the clouds.
Catching her sailors, she follows on rough sea winds,
With soft wise whispers, she sees them safely home.

PART 2

WRITING WITH YOUR MUSE

Methods of Communication

"The most beautiful thing we can experience is the mysterious; it is the source of all true art and science." Albert Einstein

Levels of Consciousness

In the film, *Dragonfly*, a nun named Sister Madeline explains to our confused, grieving hero that his recently deceased wife could be trying to contact him through children who've had near-death experiences. She suggests that his wife's spirit may meet them in a kind of tunnel and impart messages to deliver. The nun says that anesthesiologists study levels of consciousness. Between life and death are one hundred steps. At ten steps, a patient has no awareness of the surgery, so that's as far as the anesthesiologist needs to take the patient. But below are ninety more that lead into an unexplored gray area.

The mind is a mysterious creation. With so many levels of consciousness, how do we know where we are when we're communicating with spirit? When we're dreaming?

When we're tapping into our intuition? When we're on a shamanic journey into the Underworld?

Scientists have recently confirmed the conventional wisdom that you should review material for a test the night before. The best time to acquire information is right before sleep because it attaches and sticks in our memory. Why? Though we may be in beta, we're downshifting into alpha and theta.

Other sage advice is this: Don't make an important decision before you go to bed. Instead, ask it aloud before you go to bed. Then let it go. The answer will come to you, and when it does, you'll know it's right.

Between awake and asleep, there are multiple levels—a spectrum of consciousness. One thing we know is that if we don't write down our dreams while we're still in the gray zone, we'll lose them.

Most of us don't have the luxury of spending an extra hour or two in bed with our laptop or notebook right when we awaken. We're ripped out of our dreams by alarms, and we hit the ground running. We have pets, children, and jobs. Regardless, this is something to explore. How long can you stay in the gray zone? And what are the alternatives? Can you whisper a voice memo?

Meditation

The sleep state and the meditative state are similar. Both help relieve stress and bring the body into a relaxed state.

The difference is in consciousness.[1] When we practice meditation, we must stay present and aware. Our senses may send us signals. *I hear a train or birds or this music or this voice.* We may experience vivid imagery, hear music or voices, or converse with our muses. We might also do these things when we're asleep and unaware of what's happening around us, when our body is at rest and our muscles are relaxed.

Carve out a time in your day to practice. The more you practice, the more tuned and intuitive you'll become.

The "Clairs"

I mentioned the "Clairs" in the introduction. We each connect with and communicate with our muses differently. There are several ways documented in spiritual circles, but I'm going to mention the big three that we'll be working with in this book and offer some suggestions as to how to use these skills in your writing. Most people are stronger in one way than another, but you may be gifted in all three.

Clairsentience: Flashes and Feelings

Clairsentience is one of the more commonly known "clairs." We all have it to some degree and refer to it as intuition.

You might have a feeling. A sense. You might just know something. You trust those feelings and know when someone isn't being honest or doesn't have the best intentions. It's the "red flag" feeling, the one you should heed.

You can feel energy in a room or landscape. Some places may give you "the creeps," while others make you feel peaceful or inspire joy. In a room full of people, you know instinctively what's happening, who to approach, and who to avoid.

You may be empathic, so friends are constantly asking you to listen as they work through their problems. Empaths experience other people's feelings and absorb their pain. If this is you, be sure to erect boundaries and shield yourself. You don't want to take on someone else's stuff. Be aware of needy, narcissistic people or psychic vampires. If you feel drained, sick, or exhausted after talking to certain people heed the signs. Build those energy walls.

Perhaps you can sense spirits in the room. You might know where they're located. You might feel a shift in temperature—hot or cold.

Or you like walking in nature because you can feel the energy of sentient beings like trees, rocks, and water. It's calming and healing.

You might also pick up feelings and insights from objects—jewelry, antiques, artifacts, or thrift store clothing.

Where do you fall on the clairsentient scale?

Clairvoyance: Visions and Visuals

Clairvoyance means "clear seeing." In your visualization work, you've been working on your clairvoyant skills. The chakra of vision is the Third Eye. When you want to work with your visionary abilities, bring your attention there, to the center of your forehead. It's easier to slip into the theater if you close your physical eyes and open your spirit eyes.

Many people who are clairvoyant are also observant. Are you drawn to symbols, words (which are strings of symbols), images, colors, and shapes? Do you notice the way the sun hits someone's hair? Or how a shadow crosses a face? Perhaps you're struck by the gold orbs in a friend's green eyes. Or you're a visual artist.

Clairvoyants are vivid dreamers. When awake, you may slip into a daydream. I think Bastian from *The Neverending Story*[2] must be clairvoyant. At least Michael Ende, the author, could be. Perhaps, you're studying eagles in school, and the next thing you know, you're flying through the air

---

2. Ende, Michael. The Neverending Story. Ralph Manheim, translator. Dutton Books for Young Readers; Revised ed. edition (March 1, 1997)

looking down at the Earth like Bastian as he rides Falcor through Fantasia.

Some clairvoyants see lights around a person's body or color bursts in the air. I often see a halo around a person's head with my ordinary eyes while I'm chatting with them. When I write, I see movie scenes. Then, word by word, sentence by sentence, I type those images onto the page and into that first draft. I'll talk more about that in the section on "word weaving."

Clairaudience: Words and Music

Clairaudience is the power of clear listening and is associated with the throat chakra.

Do you often hear sounds, voices, words, or music playing in your head? Do you experience earworms—repeating songs that drive you mad and won't stop? Do strange songs pop into your head for no apparent reason? Perhaps one you haven't heard for twenty years?

One day I was driving with my daughter and singing a song in my head.

She said, "Oh, I like that song," and reached over to turn up the radio.

"The radio's not on," I said. "What song was it?"

"Oh, that one about time."

"If I Could Turn Back Time?"

"Yeah, that's the one. Cher sings it."

"Ah, I was singing that in my head."

Our bonds are strong. You might have a relationship where you finish the other person's sentences and know what they're going to say before they say it.

If you're a musician, it may be that you chose music because you had this gift and melodies come to you. In Irish folktales, when poets slept on the mounded tombs, they brought back faerie music—intricate tunes and long poems.

Do you hear voices? If you do, remember that words must be loving and kind. If you're replaying a previous conversation or ruminating on something, it's psychological, not spiritual. Our minds constantly push out reams of backed up conversations. This is not clairaudience. You know Spirit's talking when it's startling and it keeps returning as a message that gets louder. For example, clairaudient people often hear their name shouted by a voice that's not their own.

Writers talk about hearing words, conversations, and strings of poetry when they're doing something other than writing. Many poets write when they're out in nature. I know a mystery writer who gets his inspiration while driving around the city where his stories are set. Another author hears amazing stories in the shower. Another walks in nature every day when she's drafting a new book. I hear conversations when I go for walks or when I'm puttering around the house, cleaning and tidying, or gardening.

Now that most of us carry phones, recording an audio file is the best way to capture words and ideas.

Try This: Assess Your Gifts

"Hide not your talents. They for use were made. What's a sundial in the shade?" Benjamin Franklin

Spend some quiet time reflecting on your gifts and journaling. Ask yourself the following questions and record the answers in your journal.

Am I stronger in one area than another? How do I know? What are my strengths? As you reflect, catch memories that arise—things you've buried in the archives.

How's my meditation practice? Could I spend more time visualizing, listening, and working with all my senses?

Am I a dreamer? Do stories come to me in the night? Do I awaken with stories, scenes, words, and visions? How can I use these gifts in my writing?

Antidote to Fear: Stop Suffering

I CAN ONLY WRITE WHEN I'M SAD, ANGRY, OR EMOTIONAL. WHEN LIFE IS GOOD, I HAVE NOTHING WORTHWHILE TO SAY AND NO INSPIRATION AT ALL.

The myth of the suffering artist promotes this belief, which is more widespread than you might think. Aristotle—we're back to the Greeks again—spoke of a sense of melancholy in creative men. According to Hippocrates' humor theories, melancholy equated to the humor black bile, which was cold and dry, dark and sour, and originated in the spleen.

Western culture romanticizes the idea that artists must suffer for their work. Even die. And so, we have a host of artists, writers, and musicians whose mental and emotional suffering became their identity and ultimately ended in their early deaths. Many, like Sylvia Plath and Virginia Wolf, suffered from mental illness, and art became a means to express what couldn't be expressed any other way.

But they did not need to suffer to write. They suffered, and they wrote.

Many of us started writing in our teens when we were angry, sensitive, and fighting for independence from authority figures like our parents and their values. As rebel bards, we drew power from our differences and their indifference. And our pens acted as swords to cut us free from societal bonds. I still have reams of poetry and declarations that reflect the pain, suffering, and turmoil I experienced in ninth grade when my world imploded.

> **It's a maze, it's a haze, it's a crazy place.**
> **It's the world each day I have to face.**
> **The plastic people are insane.**
> **The atmosphere is drab. Mundane.**
> **My life is getting hard to shake**
> **And pressures round me tense to break.**
> **It's a maze, it's a haze, it's a crazy place,**
> **And as long as I live it's the world I'll face.**

Prophetic for an angsty fourteen-year-old. I still live in the same crazy world, and I still navigate it with words. But life is good. Feeling well and healthy, I write now more than ever before.

I don't need to suffer for my art, and neither do you.

Writing is a way through suffering. It's cathartic. It's healing. It gives us power through our voice. But suffering is not the only way into writing. Your muses are here to guide you. So, stop suffering and write.

Stop Thinking

"You're best when you're not in charge. The ego locks the muse."
—Robin Williams

I've done many things to connect with my muses, including going to the Underworld on a shamanic journey, offering them a place to hang out, and giving them free rein. Later, I do the hard work of getting the right words on the page alone, and then I revise and revise. But writing with your muse happens without thought. It's about igniting the initial spark. Revision is a different process. And it takes thought.

Let me say it again: When I'm tuned into the creative force, I'm not thinking. How do I know? Characters think, speak, and act in unexpected ways that surprise me. In *To Sleep with Stones*, I wrote through the deaths of two characters, wiping tears from my eyes. I had no idea they were going to die.

That's a deep connection. Thought is analytical, sometimes critical, and often judgmental. It can block the creative process. Writers who stare at blank screens are thinking. So, stop thinking and start connecting with your muse. How do you know when you're connected? Your characters will come alive. Time will stop.

Writing in your Sleep

I've suffered with insomnia for years. What I've now accepted is that night is a magical time when the muse is with me. I write in my sleep. Sometimes, I wake up with words I know I'll never remember in the morning. What do I do? Despite knowing that if I turn on the light and pick up my pen and journal, I'll be moving up a level of consciousness, I do it. I've written some amazing things in the middle of the night that blow me away when I read them the next morning. Here's a tip. Use a hazy pink salt lamp. Bright light from the sun, the computer screen, and electric lights is what wakes us up.

If lights and pens are too much, you might try voice memos on your phone. If the light on your phone is too much, set your display to dark. And, if all else fails, try telling your brain to remember. Sometimes, I can remember basic ideas in the morning. It's a far cry from what I experience at night, but it's something.

Pay Attention

In *To Kill a King*, I created a character named Ana. I wanted her to be a goddess-queen in direct opposition to my female protagonist, Sorcha.

In Celtic society, fair skin and long, flowing blonde hair were celebrated and envied. They even had a word for it—*cuilfhionn*, pronounced *coolun*. I googled images of a blonde actress with her hair elaborately braided, and I called her Ana. She was a Sun Goddess for my Sun God-King and glittered when they drove together in her chariot. But I couldn't connect with her. I'd created an image of the character *I thought she should be,* but I knew nothing about who she really was. "Who are you, Ana?" I'd ask.

The question remained unanswered while I wrote my way through two-thirds of the novel. Then, one day, my protagonist, Estrada, was engaged in a deeply emotional conversation with his lover, Michael Stryker. Estrada was also trying to understand Ana. Then Michael said, "Give the Crow Queen what she wants."

"The Crow Queen?" Estrada and I both said and suddenly there she was. Elaborately plaited indigo hair, crow feathers poking out, dark eyes, and a blackened mind. A young, power-hungry widow, Ana is a goddess to be sure, but she's no *cuilfhionn;* she's a Kali or a Morrigan.

The difference was in thinking up a character and connecting with my muse, who, in this case, was Michael, one of my regular characters.

Ah, so that's who you are! I thought. Once I connected with The Crow Queen, I understood why she was dark. I knew her backstory and her motivations. I knew about the nest of baby crows she stole as a child—the crows who acted as her spies and followed her, even killed for her.

This affected the bones of my story and everything shifted.

TRY THIS: CHOOSE A PROJECT

To me the Muses truly gave an envied and a happy lot: E'en when I lie within the grave, I cannot, shall not, be forgot. Sappho

Finding Structure

What do you really want to write? You may think you know. You may read a particular genre and think, *I can do that.* Stories may be coming to you. Or poetic lines and images. Or maybe you're empathetic and want to write a self-help book or even a cookbook that goes beyond recipes. You might be at a time in your life when a memoir is looming. Or you've written novels and want to try a screenplay.

Remember, I wrote about The Muse Within as a deep part of you, your inner source? Though your thoughts may be scattered, and you may be indecisive, your muse can help you discover what you really want.

Objectives:

- Connect with The Muse Within

- Decide on a project

Sequence

Begin by drawing your awareness to your breath, either to your rising chest and belly or the edges of your nostrils. Breathe in cool air and breathe out warm air. *Breathe in. Breathe out.* Your muscles begin to relax. Scan your body slowly from toes to crown, simply becoming aware of any places where you might be holding tension. Pay particular attention to your shoulders, neck, jaw, and tongue. If you encounter tension, just breathe it out, until you feel a sense of release, then move on. Continue to follow your breath in and out and, as you do, simply *Breathe in. Breathe out.*

Your body begins to feel heavier. You're sinking like sediment to the bottom of a pool. As your spirit clears and lifts, a soft glow forms around your body. *Breathe in. Breathe out.*

Before you stands a building with a large marquee. Your name is illuminated in swirling gold letters across the bottom. Is there a title? What kind of writing is this? A movie? A screenplay? A novel? A self-help book? A memoir? A book of poetry? You see it, you know it, or you hear it.

A door opens below the marquee, and a figure emerges. This is someone benevolent who's here to support you with your writing. This is one of your muses. Notice everything about them. Open all your senses to take them in.

This person may have a gift for you, say something, or just be.

Give them however much time and attention are needed.

Grounding: When it's time to come back, you say goodbye, knowing that you can meet them again. Pick up your pen and write down everything you've just experienced.

Before you read it over, come back fully into your body. Feel your fingers. Stretch. Send your roots down into the earth and ground.

Now you can read it over.

CHANNELED WRITING

*"One thing I know, that I know nothing.
This is the source of my wisdom."* Socrates

What is Channeled Writing?

When we're channeling, we're working at levels of consciousness separate from and deeper than ordinary rational reality. Levels we can't yet define. But we do know that channeling was practiced by seers and philosophers in the ancient Greek world, for example by Socrates, who listened to his inner voice. Later, this technique was used by authors, poets, artists, and saints. You may have heard of psychic Edgar Cayce who was known as the "sleeping prophet" or other contemporary channelers: Jane Roberts, who channels Seth, Jack Pursel, who channels Lazarus, and Pat Rodegast, who channels Emmanuel.

The intuitive voice can be captured on the page. But to access this guidance, you must practice stilling your mind through meditation. Only when you're calm and centered can you hear the intuitive voice. The more you meditate, the more sensitive you'll become.

How Do I Know It's Real?

This is a great question. There's a difference between your conscious and subconscious thoughts (the rambling of your mind and negative nagging) and the voice of deeper consciousness. It's a different voice, and you'll know intuitively when you experience it.

Automatic Writing vs. Channeled Writing

Some people refer to channeled writing as automatic writing, but it's slightly different. Automatic implies you're unaware of what's happening. Like driving down the street in your car, your brain tells your body what to do without any thought on your part. You pick up a pencil and scribble without having any awareness of what you're doing or writing. This is the case with trance channeling which is what Edgar Cayce practiced.

However, in channeled writing, although you're bypassing your rational mind, you're still aware and not completely disconnected. In that way, once you've made a connection with your muse, you can engage in a dialogue.

This isn't so much about using your clairvoyant skills as calling on your muse and listening clearly to their responses; however, your other senses may play a part. Just be aware of anything and everything and make a note.

Try This: Channeling

Objectives:

- Enter a meditative state

- Connect with one of your muses

- Ask questions and get answers in writing

Preparation:

Read over these instructions first.

Turn off the technology and set up your sacred space. Use whatever tools you resonate with—candles, incense, music, or silence— to enter a meditative mode. Have your writing tools at hand. Be warm and comfortable.

Set your intention. One must open your mind. To do that, you must surrender your doubts and fears and trust in yourself and the process. Another is to know what you want. You must ask to receive.

I find that having a specific question or list of questions helps me focus. You might ask, what do I need to know right now? Or you might ask something specific: What do I need to know about X? If you're confused about something, ask for clarity. As you dialogue, ask other questions as they arise.

You might call upon a certain muse to assist by giving you guidance. Choose whichever muse you'd like to work with—a spirit guide, a character, your deep self, or perhaps a spirit.

Don't think. Don't analyze. Don't correct. Don't stop typing or put down the pen. If you find yourself stopping, it's because you've slipped back into the rational mind. Just take a few more deep breaths, focus on your heart chakra, and begin again.

Note: It can look however you want it to. In the example that follows, I typed on my laptop. I don't use capital letters in answers because it takes me away from listening. I do use punctuation to indicate a pause or stop. You might find the vocabulary, the grammar, and even the lilt and cadence of the voice have changed. There may be things you don't understand or expect. That's the beauty of channeled writing. It's full of surprises.

Are you ready?

Sequence:

Find your still point through meditation. *Breathe in. Breathe out.* Stay there as long as you need to. Don't rush. Just breathe.

Take your attention to the space above your head and visualize a golden light funneling down from the sky and into the top of your head. It's a light, sparkling mist. Follow it from the crown chakra, through the third eye in the center of your forehead, and into your throat. This is the chakra of the creative voice. Bathe your throat with gold. Then let it float down your shoulders, arms, and hands, then through your heart and solar plexus. Finally, the mist settles below your navel in the chakra of creativity and embraces your root. Allow it to flow down your legs and feet and out into the earth. It spreads from the edges of your physical body out into your aura and fills your space with gold.

Now ask your first question, and when the first word comes, open your eyes and record the answer. One word after another, it will come. Let the words flow and, as they do, capture them on the page.

When you feel a natural ending to the conversation, stop.

Then read it back. How do you feel about the words you've written? Are you surprised by anything? Did it provide some clarity or answer the question you asked? How was the process? Did you slip easily into a meditative state or were you resistant?

Every time you do this, it will be different, so keep your channeled writings.

One Channeling Experience

Once, during a psychic reading, Joy told me that an ancient Indigenous man associated with stones, rocks, and earth was close. Later, when I was out walking, I heard a name. *Sharba*. When I wrote it, the name appeared like this: *Siarba*. I decided to do some channeled writing with him, as I was curious why he was here. This is a pleasant way to work with your spirit guides. Here's what I recorded in my digital journal.

Tell me about you, please.

shaman, healer, builder of the stones. you are right when you see the stone houses. they are ours. we traveled up and down the coastline. we built houses. we lived. weathered the storms and winds of the seas, raised our children, ate the fish, smoked the seaweed to see things when the moon was full, rattled shells and blew the horns of the sea gods.

When?

when the earth was fresh and clean and not folding in on herself. when the birds sang of stories and told us where to find the fish. when the whales came. when the world was plenty and love was full like the moon.

Are you a spirit guide?

one who loves you and feels your longing for that time. you write of it and dream of it. your dreams fold in on themselves like your earth.

Can you say more?

you feel me. my essence. i am of your gods now, your shamans. i have transcended the wheel of return and come like a flair to your energy. found you. do you wonder why you never feel alone? you are not. you are surrounded by those who love you, have loved you. in the house of stones.

Where is the house of stones?

there. (I saw a map of Skara Brae in Orkney.) when the wind came and the sea raged we walked south, crossing waters, moving, always moving, thousands of your years, but there is no time once you surpass the physical and move into spirit. don't fear it. the earth changes but spirit does not and in the ever-growing darkness there is light and love. rest.

When he said "rest," I assumed our conversation was complete, so I stopped and read over what he'd said.

I visited Orkney in 2009 and went to Skara Brae.[1] Though it's in the far north of Scotland, the Viking influence is evident. It's a fascinating sacred site, close to standing stone rings, and one I'd like to spend more time exploring psychically. Maybe one day.

---

1. https://www.historicenvironment.scot/visit-a-place/places/skara-brae/

You can read about the power of the Stones of Stenness in a fascinating article written by anthropologist and National Geographic photographer, Martin Gray. His website, sacredsites.com.[2] will lead you into a world of energetic power and mystery.

---

2. https://sacredsites.com/europe/scotland/stones_of_st enness.html

SENSORY WORD WEAVING

"Nothing can cure the soul but the senses, just like nothing can cure the senses but the soul." Oscar Wilde

Slow Down & Appreciate Each Sense

Many people connect with their muses. They hear messages or see images. They may even get the words on the page. But something is missing: the sensory descriptions that allow a reader to slip into the scene.

Word by word and phrase by phrase, a piece is written. You may know what happens and write it in a few sentences, but showing what happens is a very different thing. So SLOW IT DOWN and appreciate the senses, for your soul's sake. Here are a few techniques to increase your reader's enjoyment and your own.

Sight

Sight seems common because most of us can see. But what if you were blind and suddenly gained your sight? How would you react? How would you describe everything around you? Have you ever experienced a moment when colors seemed more vibrant? When green is shimmering emerald? When the sun on snow is blinding or so dazzling it makes you see spots.

See is a sci-fi drama series starring Jason Momoa that chronicles the plight of a tribe after a virus devastates the world and leaves all survivors blind. It's an intriguing concept, and watching characters hunt, fish, fight, flee, and interact takes the idea of blindness to a whole new level.

Write as if you were blind and suddenly regained your sight. Meld your eyes with those of your point-of-view character and use them like the lenses they are. Zoom in on the details. Zoom out for wide-angle landscapes. But don't just describe; allow your characters to respond emotionally to what they see and experience.

Sound

Sound is constantly around us, though we often ignore it. We can block out sounds with white noise, but that just adds another layer of sound. Even in true silence, our ears ring. In the darkness of the float pod, wearing earplugs to exclude all external noise, I follow the drumming of my heart as it pumps blood through my body. I think this must have been what it was like for the earliest people in the stillness of their pre-industrial world. Is this how we hear the heartbeat of Mother Earth? Sound is a sensory adaptation we cannot ignore in our writing.

As you write, climb inside the body of your character and experience everything through their senses. How a character speaks—their dialect, cadences, tones, and the sound of their voice—illuminates their character and mood. Certain sounds are associated with certain characters. For example, one of my characters is a bagpiper:

The drone began rich and low in the belly of the pipes, then swelled as the music flowed into a realm of its own—a pagan terrain of lilting trills that emerged from some past blood memory. The spirits of Dylan's ancestors swirled around them like gray ghosts in the trees, as the pipes conjured memories of ancient rebels charging into battle as well as modern heroes revered in ceremony and planted in the earth to that same gut-wrenching sound. Dylan's music could catch the human heart and wring it inside out. *To Charm a Killer*

Smell

Smell is attached to emotion and memory. Often, we smell something before we see it. Odors can trigger behaviors and/or flashbacks.

I'm sensitive to chemicals and the synthetic odors manufacturers use to mask them. The scent of fabric softener can cause my nervous system to respond as if under attack. My glands and tongue feel swollen. My fingers tremble. The muscles in my neck and throat clench, and I feel like I can't breathe or swallow. For a time, fabric softener became my kryptonite. I learned to use self-talk to regain balance. *Yes, you can smell fabric softener. Keep walking. You're safe. This will pass.* The mind is powerful; just writing about the scent of fabric softener evokes frightening memories and raises my heartbeat.

Do you know that when you read something in a book, your body responds as if you were *actually* experiencing it? Hormones are released. Systems can relax or go on high alert. This is something to remember if you like to read or write thrillers and horror novels just before bed. Do you wonder why you can't sleep? Your body may be in a fight/flight/freeze mode and emitting protective chemicals. Listening to the news creates a similar effect. Be aware of scents and odors and how they affect your mind and body.

Perfumes become associated with specific moments—be they positive or negative. Odors create associations that amplify and mingle with other senses to create feelings and behaviors.

Grandfather smelled like the rotting potatoes sprouting in the vegetable bin below the kitchen sink. She could no longer swallow mashed potatoes. They stuck in her throat like thick, grainy paste, and it took several swigs of milk to wash them down. Gravy laden potatoes were worse still. His eyes were gravy-stained, and sometimes she thought she could see them staring up at her in the mess. *Journey in Tarotia*

When the horned god, Cernunnos, comes for Sorcha at Beltane, she scents him before she sees him.

Sorcha was sleeping when his scent wafted over her, infused with everything in nature she relished most. The odor of fecund earth after a spring rain, musky wild horses, and puppy's ears, ripe peaches soaked in honeyed spices, and something else, some pheromone that awakened her desire. *To Sleep with Stones*

If your character's attacker smoked a certain tobacco, and one night she walks into her apartment and smells it, what will she do? What will happen to her physiologically? Can you climb inside her skin and write about her experience? What if she's sound asleep and her body alerts her to danger because he's entered her space and the scent has registered in her brain? Imagine awakening to the scent of your attacker in your bedroom.

Feel and Touch

Feeling and touching are two-way experiences. We don't just touch things with our fingers and receive impressions like hot or cold. Things touch us. We feel things with our bodies, but also feel things emotionally. We're affected by textures, temperatures, and preconceptions. Do you remember the old story called "The Blind Men and the Elephant" by American poet John Godfrey Saxe? Six blind men in India each touch a different part of an elephant and declare what it's like. It's like a wall, a spear, a snake, a tree, a fan, and a rope. They're all right, but all wrong because each man touched only one part and based his answer on his limited knowledge.

Taste

Taste is primal. You can taste if something is off, poisonous, salty, sour, sweet, metallic, bitter, bland, or spicy. When my nervous system is dialed up, I can taste the fabric softener as well as smell it. Taste creates visceral reactions. Think about sucking a lemon. What happens?

ESP

The Sixth Sense is Extra-Sensory Perception, and that is what this book is about. You use your sixth sense to write, but your characters can also use theirs.

When Estrada is sucked into a whirlpool off the coast of Scotland and battered by a basalt pillar. He awakens in a black cave. How are sensory experiences woven to create an emotional response? And how does his experience affect his thinking?

Estrada licked his lips and tasted blood in his parched mouth. His flesh shuddered from the cold and itched with dried salt. Battered and broken, his limbs were a mass of abrasions. He couldn't move them, and feared paralysis. He dreaded to think the worst—his back was broken beyond pain. If that was the case, his prognosis was death. A slow, malingering death. Dehydration. Delirium. Kidney failure. Coma. In a fit of exasperation, he screamed long and hard, the thunderous breaking waves outside his cell beating against his brain like Thor's hammer. If he had such a tool and could lift his hand, he would use it to bash in his own skull. *To Sleep with Stones*

FROM DRAFT TO REVISION

Writing shouldn't be scary. This isn't the final English exam that gets you into the college of your dreams. It's not going to be marked. And it's not going to determine what you'll be doing the rest of your life. It's a draft. That means nothing needs to stay as written.

The purpose of this book is to create a first draft, to get the words from the ether and onto the page. But you're not tied to them. So, relax. Nothing shuts us down faster than anxiety because it shifts us into a beta state. Be still, connect, and write your rough draft.

Once your draft is written, you begin the process of re-vision (to see it again.) Here are a few techniques to help you revise:

Use Sensory Descriptors:

DESCRIBE without using overused adjectives and clichés.

CREATE UNIQUE METAPHORS AND SIMILES that fit your genre or theme to create an association.

EMBED ARCHETYPES AND SYMBOLS.

SLIP INSIDE THE CHARACTER'S BODY and blend with them. Feel what they're feeling. Think what they're thinking.

USE LITERARY DEVICES like onomatopoeia to describe sounds.

SHOW US THROUGH A CHARACTER'S ACTIONS AND REACTIONS.

COMBINE SENSES. In the bagpipe paragraph, we can hear the drone and lilting trills, but then we move into seeing ghosts and conjuring ancestors. The characters feel it in their guts and in their hearts and are left stunned. Hopefully, the reader is too.

CREATE A PALPABLE EMOTIONAL REACTION.

USE ENHANCED DICTATION ON YOUR COMPUTER to get those words onto the page, especially if you're writing an evocative scene and the words are flowing. Enunciate clearly and speak periods and commas. Remember to proofread carefully. We've all been victims of autocorrect.

Our Friend, the Thesaurus

Once, I offended a student in one of my English classes when I asked him how much he used the thesaurus. "I never use it," he snapped. His essay was so loaded with academic, uni-level vocabulary that I thought he'd swapped every other word. It turns out he just had a high-level vocabulary. I used to tell my students not to use the thesaurus unless they knew for sure that the chosen word fit the context of the piece. Those million-dollar words sometimes scandalize us but don't correspond. They look portentous but have no signification. Having said that, a thesaurus can be used to generate inspiration. As a word nerd, I've scanned my share of dictionaries and thesauruses. The old, black hardcover tomes with gold lettering are my favorites. They smell like London libraries.

My favorite thesaurus entry is color, as there is an entire page on shades. Imagine it. Blue, ultramarine, cobalt, Prussian blue, pompadour, indigo, lapis lazuli, sapphire, turquoise, azure, cerulean, sky-blue, sea-blue, royal blue, copen, bluebird, Dresden blue, luster blue. They've forgotten good old navy and raven-wing blue. Have you ever seen a crow's feather in the sunlight? And be sure not to overuse those beautiful shades. One beta reader wrote, "You used 'azure' in the last chapter. Try something else." I use my thesaurus most when I know the word but can't bring it to mind. By looking up the closest word in meaning to what I want, I can usually find it there staring up at me smirking, "Oh, and I thought you were an English teacher."

OneLook[1] is my favorite online tool. When you're revising and your mind goes blank, you can type in a phrase to describe your thought, and up pops a host of related words. I just typed in "when you can't think of the right word" and here are a few of the suggestions: tip-of-the-tongue, lexigal gap, lethologica, mental block. Be aware that this can become its own rabbit hole. If you don't believe me, double-click on lexigal gap.

---

1. https://www.onelook.com/reverse-dictionary.shtml

Conjuring Emotions: Becoming Real

"Once you are real you can't become unreal again."
Margery Williams, *The Velveteen Rabbit*

Surprise!

Do your characters surprise you? This is a question often asked of authors. As in all things, there is a spectrum of answers depending on the individual writer's process.

At one end is the writer who says, "No. Never." This is the writer who has carefully orchestrated her plot or is perhaps confined by genre. There's no room for deviation. Allowing a character free rein, might result in something unexpected and unwelcome.

At the other end of the spectrum is the writer who has created characters, or at least acknowledged them when they've come calling, but doesn't really know how things will go. She'd rather feel her way through it than think it out. She allows the characters to make their own choices, speak out, act, and tell her what happens and why.

This requires trust because your plot can go sideways in an action-reaction sequence. Imagine what would happen if you were writing a romance with the expected "happy ever after" ending, and one of the characters did something unexpected like cheating or, even worse, got killed driving home from a stag? I dated a man once whose fiancee died in a car crash on the way home from a fitting of her wedding dress. Tragedies may occur in real life, but don't write them into your romance novel unless you're Nicholas Sparks, and heartbreak is your specialty.

Live characters create intense drama because the surprise and raw emotion experienced by the writer when a character does something unexpected translates to the page.

This free-wheeling trust may not apply to all characters. Minor characters may be plugged in to perform a function. Also, it depends on your stage in a series. Your relationships with characters in your first book, when you're still at the "getting to know you" stage will be different than those in your third book. It's like any long-term relationship. Things evolve. Trust develops. Sometimes you part ways, and we all know what happens to a character who angers the writer.

Character freedom requires the same kind of trust that's needed when you're doing psychic work. You allow spirit to work through you in the form of a character. Your job as a storyteller is to conjure emotion in your reader. No matter what kind of story you're writing, the best emotions are raw and visceral—love, hate, sorrow, fear, longing, desire, jealousy, or guilt.

How I Use It:

In *To Sleep with Stones*, I created a minor character named Christophe. He's a young French model that Michael Stryker starts seeing when Estrada abandons him (yet again) to go rescue Dylan in Scotland. Christophe is just a boy-toy to Michael, who's hurt, lonely, and acting out, so I didn't spend much time getting to know him. However, he became an antagonist with his own agenda. Note: Every character needs motivation and a goal to drive their actions.

Michael doesn't know Christophe any better than I do. He's caught up in his own narcissistic drama and the fresh gloss of a young man (a younger version of Estrada) who will give him anything he wants (sex, drugs, pain, or pleasure).

But Christophe is in love, and he's devised a plan to make Michael his forever lover. To this end, he hires a yacht, and the two men take a private cruise up the Pacific coast. At their secret destination, he promises to reveal his ultimate gift. *Vampire.* He never considers that Michael might reject his gift, steal the vampire's million-dollar yacht, and escape.

I have no control over Michael Stryker, whose alter ego, Mandragora, thinks he's the reincarnation of Lord Byron. Nobody does. I've written him for several years, during which time he's done whatever he liked. And, though they're best friends and lovers, Estrada has no control over Michael either. So, I'm not surprised by Michael's violent reaction to catching Christophe on the yacht after he escapes. Michael's winning until the enraged vampire arrives. Not only has Michael stolen his yacht, but he's also assaulted his favorite procurer—a young man the vampire considers a son.

Setting comes into play here, as setting, character, and plot are all intertwined. A vicious storm arrives at dawn. The vampire orders Christophe to drive the yacht back to his lair in this horrific gale. Then he locks Michael in a coffin, pockets the key, and climbs into another coffin to rest.

I didn't realize the scene would play out as it did. I didn't plan it. I just switched into Christophe's point-of-view and felt what he was feeling—trapped between his would-be lover and the man he considered his father. He's terrified that Michael will die, and he's equally terrified that he'll die himself because he's so inexperienced at piloting a yacht. He knows the vampire's human son died in a storm just like this in the late 1700s. I closed my eyes and typed while watching this poor man hang onto a floating coffin in the Pacific Ocean. As I wrote the scene, I was so blended with Christophe that I cried.

Here's the passage:

Christophe stood on the deck, hair flying like Medusa's snakes in the burgeoning wind. First rain, and then hail, erupted from the black sky, decreasing visibility, and increasing his anxiety. He'd come outside to see just how close he was to the shoreline. Very close. Too close. On his way back, he passed the red oak coffin that imprisoned Mandragora.

Gripping the controls, Christophe tried to maneuver the yacht away from the shoreline and into the oncoming wind. The problem was that the westerlies kept blowing it into shore, and he was driving so slowly the yacht could gain no momentum. Yet, he was afraid to drive any faster. Perhaps, he should stop and let down the anchor? The roaring of the wind and waves assaulted his ears. He trembled. Mandragora knew how to drive a yacht. If only Don Diego had not padlocked the coffin. A flash of lightning illuminated the vampire's coffin in the master cabin as if to say, I know what you are thinking. Could he perceive a man's thoughts even in his daily rest?

Suddenly the wind caught the yacht broadside. It lurched sideways and water surged over the deck. Christophe screamed. What to do? Was it dark enough in the cabin to open Don Diego's coffin and extract the key? Could he free Mandragora without hurting his Padrino? Liquor bottles hurtled from the bar smashing against walls and windows. Cupboards opened, casting out their contents, as glass and china shattered in the chaos. And then, the boat tilted.

Mandragora's coffin slid across the floor.

Running, clutching, Christophe sprawled across the red oak lid. "I will get the key," he cried.

But getting there was impossible. The boat pitched so far sideways, he could only reach the cabin by grasping furniture and hauling his body up; and alas, Christophe had no upper body strength. When finally, he fought and won and hung against the doorway of the stateroom, he glanced back, only to see Mandragora's coffin afloat. The sliding door at the back of the yacht had come ajar and water gushed in. The posh salon was flooded.

When the realization struck him, Christophe laughed at the absurdity of it. He was going to drown alone, while the two men he loved most in the world floated in sealed coffins.

After releasing the door frame, he staggered back across the salon through frigid seawater, and grasped the brass handles of Mandragora's coffin. Clinging to it with all his strength, his body trembling. The water was so cold, so deep. Laying his head against the wet wood, he heard the pounding fists, the terrified cries, but could do nothing.

"I will not leave you, chéri," he cried.

And then the boat flipped.

The will to live overcame Christophe's fear, and he swam and fought his way to the surface. He was so cold, so tired, fighting desperately to remain afloat in water that churned around him, when all he wanted was for it all to end. When a coffin hit him in the back, he used what little strength he had remaining to hoist himself on top and cling there — chest flat against the wood, heart slowing, numb fingers clutching the handles at either side, and drifting like so much flotsam and jetsam in the storm.

Christophe would not leave his lover; would not abandon him to die alone.

It was an hour before he realized that the coffin he clung to was black. Don Diego slept below him, not Mandragora. The man he loved was somewhere lost in the tempest. When the truth of this sunk into his heart, the young Frenchman bit through his lip until he tasted his own blood. And then, prying his stiff frozen fingers from the brass handles, Christophe slid off the coffin and into the sea. — *To Sleep with Stones*

Character as Muse:

When your character becomes real, your writing life will change. If you trust in your character's spirit, they will do much of the creative work for you. They might provoke a fight, defend themselves, have an indiscrete sexual moment or several, fall in love, sacrifice themselves to save someone else, or commit suicide. They might make stupid mistakes or surprise you with their utter brilliance. They will take you places you could never conceive of, where you will see things you never dreamed of seeing.

What a real character won't do is sit still and be boring. When your character becomes your muse, it takes the pressure off you, as a writer, to control them. Everyone, including your characters, is walking their own path, and to take away their freedom robs them of their internal growth. Moreover, you'll grow because of them.

Estrada, whom I've known since the beginning, has taken me to Ireland, Scotland, and up the Pacific coast. Physically and spiritually. We travel together. Do I trust him? Absolutely. Estrada is, as his good friend, Daphne says, "one of the good guys."

Recently, we time-traveled to Iron Age Ireland and back again. Estrada is as real as anyone else I know. I've felt his pain, his joy, his fear, his grief, his guilt, his love, and his lust. When I tried to put down my Hollystone Mysteries series once and write a brand-new book with a brand-new cast, I couldn't do it. I missed him too much. A third of the way through that novel, I called out, "Estrada, where are you?" The next morning, I saw the first scene of *To Kill a King*. I knew exactly where he was and what he was doing, and I knew I was writing the wrong book. That's how we ended up in Iron Age Ireland on a mission to save a lovesick archaeologist from a king destined to be ritually murdered and sunk in a bog.

Don't think Estrada controls me. Ours is a relationship of mutual free will, and he has no more sway over me than anyone else in my life.

Show Don't Tell

Delete The Adverbs and Show Emotions

Something you've probably heard from every writing teacher you've ever met is "show don't tell." But showing emotions can be challenging. It's much easier to add an adverb to the speech tag or tell your reader just how your character feels. "He said angrily" or "she felt disgusted." This is one thing that reveals your writing skills. Here are a few suggestions:

WATCH DRAMATIC FILMS AND TELEVISION SERIES to observe how the actors reveal emotions that match dialogue. I use close captioning so I can see words and actions in tandem. Watch to learn. I've seen several visceral dramas lately where a terrified character vomits. Intense internal feelings project via the viscera. Shakespeare knew this during the Renaissance and created plays laced with scatological humor. His audience knew that when a life was threatened it wasn't always possible to keep all fissures corked. In *To Render a Raven* when Estrada discovers that his baby girl's been abducted from her crib, the burritos he's just wolfed down come back up. Visceral shows it every time. Check out *Frontier* and *Peaky Blinders*.)

Keep a journal of your own emotional reactions. When do you get stomach aches or headaches? Why do you clench your teeth? Do your hands shake when you're nervous? Do you blush when embarrassed? One of my characters flushes to the tips of his ears. When does your mouth go dry? When do you look someone in the eye and when do you avert their gaze? Do you twirl your hair when you're tired? Do you have a tic or nervous giggle? People reveal emotional reactions in various ways.

Use personal experiences. We all experience conflict. How do you react? When faced with a bully or a threat, what's your usual reaction? Do you freeze, fight, or fly? If you were a different size or gender, how would you act or react differently? Have you ever *been* the bully or the threat? Where did you get your bravado? How did it feel?

Invest in online tools. I love the Writers Helping Writers Thesaurus Series by Angela Ackerman and Becca Puglisi.[1] Especially useful in this discussion is *The Emotion Thesaurus* where the writers list physical signals, internal sensations, mental responses, long term responses and cues that someone is suppressing a particular emotion. *The Emotional Wound Thesaurus: a Writer's Guide to Psychological Trauma* can help you understand your character's choices and behavior; as well as, create a rich backstory. You may not reveal it, but you should know it.

---

1. https://writershelpingwriters.net/

Characters

"I empty my mind of thoughts and cares and sink into a peaceful place where characters' names and even lines of dialogue have fluttered past." C.J. Papoutsis, author of "Leandra"

People read to escape, to live vicariously, to learn something new, to resonate with place and culture, and to root for a hero. We love an underdog who suffers to win. Think about Harry Potter, the orphaned boy who lives under the stairs in the home of his abusive aunt, uncle, and cousin. J.K. Rowling's stories follow the mythic hero's journey, which is one of the reasons they're so popular.

But we also like real-world characters who grow up in ordinary families and have extraordinary triumphs. We like to identify with characters because when they win, we win too.

If you're writing a memoir, you are the main character, so you'll need to show what makes you worthy of your own story. You don't need to slay a monster, but you do need to change and perhaps overcome something.

In your writing journal, make a list of your favorite book characters and then ask yourself why you're drawn to this particular hero.

You must give your readers a believable character who's damaged enough to make them compelling. Fiction readers want to see someone with a seemingly insurmountable task take on the monster, whoever or whatever that may be, and win.

Main Character Essentials

Main characters, be they human, animal, or fantastical, need to be *compelling*. You can't resist following their journey because they've caught your interest. How do you do this as a writer?

GIVE THEM A SPECIAL SKILL OR TALENT. Be sure to mention it near the beginning of the story so they can demonstrate it when times get tough. If you want your young woman to physically fight her villain, either send her to defense classes or mention how her dad trained her to box when she was a kid. Don't just suddenly have her jump into a brawl.

GIVE THEM A PROBLEM, A MISSION, A QUEST, AND MOTIVATION. What drives a story is *conflict*. The protagonist wants something. The antagonist wants to stop them from getting it. The best problems have serious consequences: life or death, freedom or imprisonment, love or loss. These are visceral oppositions that catch us in the gut, break our hearts, and give us hope.

GIVE YOUR CHARACTER AN INNER EMOTIONAL PROBLEM that readers can identify with—a problem that could shackle them in their quest. This helps make the character identifiable. Their "stuff" derives from their backstory and will affect their behavior, their choices, and their actions. And the most potent stuff involves secrets, guilt, and shame. Check out *The Emotional Wound Thesaurus* for inspiration.

MAKE THEM FLAWED IN SOME WAY. Shakespeare's tragic heroes all had a fatal flaw—a personality trait that led to their downfall. The fatal flaw is a feature of Greek drama which they called *hamartia* from the Greek word *hamartanein*, which means "to err." Estrada's flaw is that he falls in love hard and fast, and usually with the wrong people. It makes him interesting, often irritating, and drives his actions.

MAKE YOUR CHARACTER LIKABLE IN SOME WAY. Readers don't warm to narcissistic, self-centered fools unless they see potential for change. Screenwriter Blake Snyder calls this the *Save the Cat* rule. He suggests that if your hero is not likable, have them rescue a cat that's caught up in a tree. Show us their hearts, and their willingness to do something good.

SHOW A CHARACTER ARC OVER THE COURSE OF THE STORY. The hero changes due to events in the story that they have sparked. You can write a story about the girl next door if you include these things.

Here's an Example:

In *To Charm a Killer*, Maggie Taylor first appears as an ordinary seventeen-year-old girl in her final year of high school. Maggie goes to class, writes English essays, and walks her dog in the park. There's nothing extraordinary there. Until a sexy priest flirts with her. And her dog hears bagpipes, runs off into the woods, and disturbs a coven of witches in the midst of their Equinox ritual. When Maggie vaults over the fence after her dog, she reveals her special talent. She's a gymnast, and that skill will help her survive eventually.

What's her inner problem? Maggie wants to escape the prison that her home life has created and leave her boring life in Vancouver.

Their lives were so well constructed that Maggie had told only two people—who absolutely required an explanation at the time—that her father suffered from a severe head injury and required medication and constant monitoring to keep up the facade. She had told no one that she was the cause of that injury. —*To Charm a Killer*

Don't you want her to escape? Don't you want to know how she caused her father's injury? Aren't you hoping she'll get involved with these witches, somehow change her life, and finally be free of guilt? When Maggie gets caught up in the witches' charm, her life changes dramatically, which is what drives the plot. In this "coming of age" story, we watch her move from innocence to experience.

TRY THIS: CONJURE A CHARACTER

"While we think we are imagining a character, we may, so marvelous are the hidden ways, be really interpreting a being actually existing, brought into psychic contact with us by some affinity of sentiment or soul." Æ, pseudonym for Irish poet, artist, and mystic, George William Russell

Æ's quote reminds me of my experience in mediumship when the reader described my main character, Estrada, as if he were real—which, of course, he is.

Some characters appear fully formed and we need only record their exploits. Others require an invitation. Still others need to be coaxed into being. Take some time now and try it.

Sequence:

Gather your journal-writing tools. Open your journal and have your pen at hand. Either sit cross-legged or in a chair with your feet flat on the floor and your back straight. Close your eyes and take a few deep breaths, in through your nose and out through pursed lips. Then just breathe normally and bring your awareness to the air flowing in and out of your nostrils. Feel the muscles in your body relax—your shoulders, neck, and jaw. If thoughts intrude, notice and let them go. Don't rush. Give yourself time to clear your mind.

Keeping your eyes closed, continue to relax your body and breathe.

Ask to meet a character, then continue to follow your breath as it flows in and out.

When thoughts or images occur, open your eyes and freely write whatever comes to mind.

A parade of characters from books and films may pass through your consciousness first as you sink into a deeper focus. You may see or hear them, or a description might flow from your pen. Don't think or analyze. Just let it all arise from your consciousness and catch it on your page. If a new character appears, record everything. You could even sketch.

Antidote to Fear: No Time

I GET IDEAS, BUT DON'T HAVE TIME TO WRITE THEM DOWN IN ANY KIND OF FORM. I HAVE A JOB, CHILDREN, ANIMALS, RESPONSIBILITIES...

Writing can be a juggling act. I wrote most of this in my head while walking my dog in the woods. As I get these words on the page, I'm combining ingredients for a chocolate quinoa cake. Line by line. Hang on a second . . . Okay, I'm back. The cake's in the oven, and the timer is on.

"I don't have time" is a form of procrastination. If you believe you don't have time to write, you won't. Instead, try the following suggestions:

USE A TIMER. I don't know how many pots of quinoa I've burned. Or rice. Or potatoes, which are the absolute worst thing to burn dry on the stove. Use a timer when you're cooking, but also to remind yourself of YOUR time to work. *I'm going to meditate for ten minutes. I'm going to work on my manuscript for the next two hours without checking social media.*

BLOCK OUT YOUR WRITING TIME AND SEND YOURSELF NOTIFICATIONS. If you had a job that earned you $200 an hour, you'd show up and put in the time, right? Writing is just as important. Don't relegate writing to the last thing you do. You'll never get there.

DON'T ANSWER THE PHONE, AND LET PEOPLE KNOW WHEN YOU'RE UNAVAILABLE. How many of you have family and friends that think, "Oh, she works at home. She's not busy." Then, they call you and chat for an hour of your writing time. This isn't their fault. It's your responsibility to set boundaries. Screen calls. Let people leave a message. It's easy to be distracted by your cell phone. I think this is why people write in coffee shops. If I know my friend writes in the morning, I save my thoughts until the afternoon. That's being respectful. But also show yourself respect by telling people that you write in the morning or whatever is the best time for you.

GO WRITE IN COFFEE SHOPS. If you can handle the noise (I can't), a coffee shop can be your office. Just make sure you do all the other things listed here while you're sitting in the coffee shop, or you'll find yourself either talking on the phone or sucked into the social media vortex.

UNPLUG. Ah, yes. The aforementioned social media vortex. As a writer, you're expected to promote and market yourself. That means contributing to social media on a regular basis. Notice I said contributing to and not spending hours reading, liking, and commenting on everyone else's posts. You need to do your share, but don't get sucked down the rabbit hole.

CHECK YOUR EMAIL LIKE YOU WOULD CHECK YOUR SNAIL MAIL. Once a day is fine. This is another one of those drains, like texting.

We've turned Pavlovian. Every time we hear a beep or a notification drifts across our screen, we jump into action. Revolt.

CHOOSE YOUR ACTIVITIES WISELY. It's important to keep up your professional development as a writer, and that means going to writers' groups, festivals, and conferences. Not only do you meet people, but you also get inspired. So, do try to block out time for annual author celebrations and whatever else you can manage. I know several writers who meet up regularly on Zoom to offer support to each other.

JOIN A GROUP THAT OFFERS WRITING SPRINTS. I can recommend the Creative Academy for Writers.[1] They're a dedicated group of supportive writers, working in myriad genres all over the world, who offer online sprint rooms for people to work. They don't talk or socialize in the room. They just write. The times are posted, so you know in advance when you're unavailable.

LIMIT YOUR TELEVISION TIME. This is another great place to use a timer. Or try a natural timer. I often watch my favorite Peter Gabriel concert on Youtube (Secret World 1994) and sing and dance while I'm cooking. Since Peter Gabriel is one of my muses, this doesn't count as wasted time. Well, maybe I'm stretching that a little. I try to avoid binge-watching my favorite Netflix series, but I'll admit, I'm not always successful. Again, don't be too hard on yourself if you're watching something in your genre. A part of your brain will be analyzing how the screenwriters created that dynamite plot twist, or applied the "hero's journey," or how is this

---

1. https://creativeacademyforwriters.com/

movie one of the ten types Blake Snyder describes in *Save the Cat*. This turns TV time into professional development time. Mind you, if you're watching reruns of "The Big Bang Theory," you might want to have a chat with yourself. That was my signal to take a teaching leave and become a lighthouse keeper.

EXPLAIN TO YOUR PEOPLE HOW IMPORTANT WRITING IS TO YOU AND ASK FOR THEIR SUPPORT. Women, in particular, are still holding down jobs and looking after homes and families, while trying to write. Several women authors found success writing for a few hours in the evening when the house was quiet and their muses were speaking. Margaret Laurence, for one, and Diana Gabaldon, for another. I completed university as a single mother and then wrote the first two Hollystone Mysteries while I was working full time as a secondary school teacher. It can be done. But you must set priorities and be honest with yourself. If your friends don't support your writing dreams, it's time to rethink relationships.

INVEST IN WRITING SOFTWARE that will help you stay organized. I held off buying Scrivener[2] for years. I didn't want to have to learn another software program. Now I use it for drafting and organizing my research, and I've found it to be a timesaver. More on that in the chapter called "Research & Records."

---

2. https://www.literatureandlatte.com/

On the subject of software, I also recommend Atticus,[3] a publishing program for Indie authors. I'm using it right now to format and edit this book. I used to write and format all my books in Word, which took hours and hours of writing time, and a change had to be made in three different files. Atticus offers several customizable themes so you can write and format your book, then export a PDF for print and an epub for digital platforms. That's one file to change if you discover an error, and that will save you time.

---

3. http://atticus.io

Try This: Interview a Character

Objectives:

- Conjure/channel a character

- Ask them specific questions and receive information

- Try to discover their name

I love this word, conjure. It means to bring into existence or cause to appear as if by magic to the eye or mind; to evoke; to perform tricks that are seemingly magical; to call upon a spirit to appear. And so, we'll slip into a meditative state and see which character is waiting to be conjured into existence. Then we'll ask them questions using the channeling process.

Preparation:

Write down your questions before you begin, but be prepared to flow with the conversation. You may see the character in your mind's eye. If you do, jot down details or sketch them. You may hear something—a name, music, a distinctive voice, tone, or vocal pattern, or a laugh. Just flow with it. Don't think. Trust in the intuitive process. Think of what it's like to meet someone for the first time. How do you begin a conversation? Perhaps pretend you're a counselor. As you write down questions, remember the essentials you need to create a character. Here are a few possibilities:

Do you have a best friend? What are they like? (Sometimes it's easier to start by talking about someone else, and you might find they have a sidekick.)

What are your favorite colors? Animals? Sports? Books? Movies? (Small talk.)

What do you like to do? What are your passions? (Get them excited.)

Do you have a special skill or talent? (Appeal to ego.)

How are things going in your life? Are you happy? Sad? Confused? Angry? Tell me why you're here. Remember, you need to know their inner problem, and their backstory. Get to the heart of it.

Do you have a secret? What's something you've never told anyone?

What's your name? (I purposely left this to last so you don't feel pressured.)

Sequence:

Find your still point through meditation. *Breathe in. Breathe out.* Stay there as long as necessary. Don't rush. Just breathe. Take your attention to the space a few inches above your head and visualize a golden light funneling down from the sky and into the top of your crown. It's a beautiful golden mist. Follow it from the crown chakra, through the third eye in the center of your forehead, and into your throat. This is the chakra of the creative voice. Bathe your throat with gold. Then let it float down your shoulders and hands, and through your heart and solar plexus. Finally, the mist settles below your navel in the chakra of creativity and embraces your root. Allow it to flow down your legs and feet and out into the earth. It spreads from the edges of your physical body into your aura and fills it with gold.

Now open your eyes enough to see and pick up your pen. Ask your first question, and record the answer. One word after another, it will come. Let the words flow and, as they do, capture them on the page.

A Note About Names:

Writing a book is like having a baby, and naming a character is like naming your child. Such a big piece of their identity should fit with their look and personality. Think Hannibal

Lecter, Lord Voldemort, Uriah Heep, Cruella de Vil, Dr. Jeckyl, or Professor Moriarty. Okay, they're all villains. But you get my point. There's no need to be subtle with names. I feel that some of J. K. Rowling's success with *Harry Potter* is due to her choice of character names—Hagrid, Professor Dumbledore, Draco Malfoy, Severus Snape, Grindelwald, Weasley, Hermione—the names themselves are memorable.

A name can be symbolic, whispered by a character, or pulled from the air. Other times the name doesn't come, and I scan lists of the most popular baby names by country and decade and roll them around on my tongue. I like rhythm and sound, assonance, and alliteration. Often, I jot down names that strike me. Estrada was the last name of one of my English students long ago, and I liked it as soon as I heard it. "I'm going to name a character Estrada one day," I said. And I did.

Don't be disappointed if a name doesn't arrive with a character. All you can do is ask. You're the parent, and you can name your child whatever you like. Unless they have a different idea as they come into their power.

If Your Muse Disappears

"I would especially like to re-court the Muse of poetry, who ran off with the mailman four years ago, and drops me only a scribbled postcard from time to time." John Updike

From time to time, you might find yourself in a place where you're not writing or even thinking about writing. It's like your muse has packed their bag and gone on vacation. This is different from writer's block, which happens when you really want to write, but can't find the inspiration or get the words down on paper. I'm talking about times when you stop thinking about writing at all.

This can happen if your schedule is too tight, your mind is too full, or your emotional life is too chaotic. Sometimes you just need time to recharge, and your muse knows it. The connection between you and your muse breaks, thereby halting the flow of creativity and inspiration. It's not a bad thing, and it won't last forever.

I've experienced this myself. One moment, I was feeling amazing. I'd just written to a friend, "I feel happier and healthier than I've felt in years!" And I meant it. Fifteen minutes later, I went to see my doctor for my annual physical. She told me she felt a lump in my breast. She said she didn't think it was anything to worry about, but I should have a mammogram because *it could turn into cancer in two months*. I'm not exaggerating. Those were her words. When you hear the words, *I feel a lump,* you remember everything.

I immediately went into a beta state, and called both my naturopath and my traditional Chinese medicine doctor to get their opinions. Both said that having a mammogram wasn't a bad idea. It might ease my mind.

At the time, I was two weeks away from a huge move. Don't these things always happen at inopportune times? So I put off the appointment. Really, I didn't want to go. Mammograms frighten me, so I'd never had one. That's why my doctor tried to scare me into action. But hospitals scare me more; in fact, the whole western medical profession scares me. If you write suspense, you know that *not* knowing is far scarier and more anxiety-producing than knowing. Still, I put it off.

I started doing affirmations, long visualization sessions, and pendulum work, and I called on my spirits to support me in cleansing and healing my body. Weeks went by where the fear of cancer seemed to always be in the back of my mind. This was the hardest thing for me because I believe that we manifest the things we focus on. I didn't want to create cancer by thinking about it. But I couldn't help but think about it.

I stopped writing, although I had a romantic suspense novel in progress. I moved and settled somewhat, and I finally forced myself to make an appointment for the dreaded mammogram. One of my biggest fears was being told I needed more tests or treatments. I didn't want to open that door. When I called to make the appointment at the end of September, they informed me that my doctor had referred me for both a mammogram and an ultrasound. I ended up having them both in the same week. Then I waited. Tick tock. More suspense.

A week later, my doctor's office called to report that there was nothing abnormal in my mammogram. The ultrasound showed no lump or mass—nothing at all. *Phew.* Then another thought. *What happened? Did Spirit cleanse it from my body? Did those affirmations work?*

The next morning, I awoke at 5:30 a.m. with the whole back half of my work in progress playing through scenes in my head. It was like I was in the theater watching the movie. I grabbed my journal and pen from the bedside table and started scrawling. Characters I hadn't thought about in almost two months were showing me their next moves. I write from multiple viewpoints and could suddenly see how five different characters' actions and motivations were interconnected, and I knew they'd all come together for the climax.

Once I had the notes on paper, I was able to use them to write full scenes. When the veil of anxiety lifted, my muses could get through. Perhaps they'd been speaking all along, and I couldn't hear them. Perhaps they knew I wasn't in the right space to accept what they had to say. Perhaps they were working hard for me in a different way by providing me with healing.

Remember when we talked about brain waves? I spent most of the time in the story I just told enmeshed in beta waves. During my sojourns into healing visualizations and working with my spirits, I dipped into alpha, but I never stayed long enough to connect with my characters, and my focus was on healing. I may even have been writing in my sleep, unaware of having delta dreams. It was only when I was able to free my mind from worry that I was able to hear and see my muses again.

Has your muse ever run off? Do you remember a time you lost connection with your muse and stopped thinking about writing? What were you doing? What kind of space were you in? What was the trigger?

Open your writing journal and explore this topic with as much detail as possible, like I just did. Ask yourself what was happening in your life. How did it end? Did you wake up one day and start writing again? If you're in this space right now, how can you free up your mind so you can connect with your muses?

ANTIDOTE TO FEAR: JUDGMENT

IF MY MOTHER READS WHAT I WRITE, SHE'LL BE SO APPALLED SHE'LL NEVER SPEAK TO ME AGAIN.

When I was a rebellious teenager, I kept a small red diary with a little gold lock. I used to write exciting things in that diary in graphic detail. Some were true. Some were not. Most were sexy. After all, I was a teenage writer. And if you've read Shakespeare, you know that literature is mostly about love, sex, and death, along with a few other things like betrayal and who makes the best king. Like many teens, I'd experienced love, sex, and death by the time I was fifteen.

I still remember the day my mother waved that diary in my face. She'd searched my room. When she found it, she picked the little gold lock and read it, and no doubt shared it with my father. At fifteen, I was my parents' greatest fear.

When the yelling and the disapproving looks ended, I got that little red book back. Clutching it in my fist, I took off into the forest. Nature, for me, has always been a place of refuge. There, I sat alone among the trees, ripping out those offending pages and burning them. I learned a few things that day in the sulfurous glow of getting caught.

That experience created negative beliefs about writing. I didn't keep another diary for years. The next time I wrote something acutely personal in a journal, it was during an Indigenous Studies class, and I was writing to heal. I was much older, in my thirties. We'd been discussing secrets and their power. My professor had created a safe space between him and me where I felt comfortable enough to write about things that had happened to me as a teenager—those #metoo moments that were still impacting me.

Sometimes revealing a personal secret is like popping a balloon. If you're still standing after the initial bang, your heartbeat will slow, and you'll be able to move forward. Many of us write to heal and use art to explore our trauma.

As for my mother . . . Now that I'm older, I know she would *love* my books, especially the sexy ones. She had her own share of sexy books lined up on her bookcase headboard. *Messalina* and *Peyton Place* were my eleven-year-old favorites. My mother loved adventures and mysteries. She might gasp a little and gloss over the word *fuck*—she once broke a plate when she was washing dishes and I asked her what *fuck* meant—but I know she'd keep reading. She'd love my protagonist, Estrada, and she'd appreciate the journeys he takes to save his friends and family.

Plus, it's not the voice of her teenage daughter, who may or may not be experiencing the things she's writing about. Now I write fiction. Do I have concerns about being judged? Yes, it happens sometimes. After all, I do write sexy LGBTQ urban fantasy books. But the fear of judgment hasn't stopped me from writing and, ironically, most of my audience is composed of women who are mothers.

PART 3

DIVING DEEPER WITH YOUR MUSE

RESEARCH & RECORDS

I don't want to give you the impression that my writing is based solely on dreams, spiritual interventions, and magic. Writing is work, and research is key to drafting a detailed, credible story. I do a tremendous amount of research before and during my first draft, and all that information must be kept somewhere logical so I can retrieve it when needed.

Working with Scrivener

Research styles are as unique as record-keeping systems. Writers might use paper and file cabinets, shoe boxes, Ikea boxes, binders, or files and bookmarks in their browsers. As I mentioned, I find Scrivener[1] useful at the creation stage. It's a powerful word processor. Imagine a virtual binder where you upload research, keep character bios, draft your book in scenes and chapters, and then compile it into a document. I don't use all the features available in Scrivener,

---

1. https://www.literatureandlatte.com

but a few I find useful are manuscript, corkboard, and character/setting templates.

Manuscript

When you open "manuscript" you can write a chapter or a scene. It's important to save your work after each session. I save it to a work in progress file on my computer and back it up to an external drive. Be aware that every time you save, you end up with a new version that's stamped with date and time, so when you pick it up again, make sure you're using the most recent document.

Once I've completed my first draft, I "compile" it to a Word document so I can send it to an editor or upload it to Atticus[2] my new formatting software. I might be boggling your mind with so many software programs, especially if you're not comfortable with technology, but each of them has a purpose.

Corkboard

"Corkboard" is a unique feature in Scrivener. Here, you'll find a moveable card for each scene where you can note: point-of-view, date, time, setting, and a few key sentences to explain what happens and why. Not everyone writes in sequence, so it's a handy way to record ideas for scenes and shift them around. Later, you can transform your corkboard notes into an outline, which is useful when you need to write a synopsis.

---

2. https://www.atticus.io/

Character and Setting Templates

I usually create a template for each character so I can easily find information to use as I draft. I include their name and its meaning; age, date of birth, astrological sign, and sometimes Myers-Briggs personality type,[3] place of residence, a physical description, the character's goal, emotional wounds and backstory, habits, plus internal and external conflicts that relate to the story. I haven't used setting much, but I can see how it could be useful to download maps and jot down related characters, features, and sensory descriptors. Also, it would be good to note what happens where and why.

Combining Intuition and Research

Once I've conjured a character, I often have a name and a basic description. I know who they'll be connected to in the story and if they're helpful or antagonistic—someone who tries to sidetrack the protagonist. In the Hero's Journey, they're known as "allies" and "enemies." I sometimes create a sociogram as a graphic organizer when I'm reading a novel for review or writing a draft, so I can keep track of names and relationships. A simple way is to write the title in the center and add circles with the character' names and lines to join them. You can add other notes if you like.

When I was drafting *To Charm a Killer* years ago, I taped a huge blank piece of paper up on my wall. I started with a sociogram and then added photographs and other key

---

3. https://www.16personalities.com/

information, such as symbols. As I worked, a unique mural unfolded. If you're artistic, hands-on, or prefer analog to digital, this might serve you. I always envisioned the fey witch Primrose as a young Sinéad O'Connor, so her image is front and center.

How it Works

In book five, I created a couple who are related to Sorcha O'Hallorhan through backstory. Sorcha is one of the main characters in three of my books. Their relationships crystallized when I started musing about Sorcha's emotional wounds. One woman was her best friend; the other, her ex-lover.

In the previous book, the characters had traveled backwards in time to prehistoric Ireland, and at the beginning of book five, they've just ridden back through a wormhole on horseback into present-day Ireland. They're home, sort of. With no ID, cash, credit cards, or mobile phones, they're stuck in peat-mined County Offaly. Sorcha hopes these two women, who own a nearby stable, can mind the horses and loan her enough cash to purchase a mobile and some fake IDs. With that knowledge, I set about creating a backstory for the three women that would affect their current story and spur conflict. That's where the research comes in.

I needed to know about equestrian stables close to Croghan Hill so my characters could walk or ride there. For that, I needed maps. I used both Google Earth and Google Maps. I knew there were horse farms and stables in County Kildare, as I'd gone horseback riding there years ago. So, I went through a list of stables and located them on my maps. Using the "walk" feature in Google Maps, I was able to plot a path to a fictional stable in a real town that my characters could reach in a few hours. I often choose towns and names by sound, so Lullymore became my target. Lullymore has such a lilt; it has to be a special place.

Then, I needed last names, family histories, and a timeline that fit with information already published in other books that featured Sorcha. I knew that I'd mentioned how she was fourteen years old in 2003 when Old Croghan Man had been dug from the peat in Co. Offaly at the base of Croghan Hill. Later, I mentioned that a climactic event occurred in Greenland in 208 BCE—an event Sorcha remembered because she'd read about it in 2008, her first year in university. So, those events formed the basis of my timeline, and I worked from there.

I also needed to flesh out the two women Sorcha knew from the National University of Ireland in Galway, a place I've actually visited. And I needed to know what transpired between these three women to cause their estrangement eight years ago. Then I asked: How will past events at the university color their meeting now?

I set up a new character template in Scrivener and searched the Internet for answers to my questions. I also pulled up a photograph of an actress who resembled an image of one of the women I envisioned. From there, I was able to discern her emotional wounds, internal conflicts, and current state of mind. With all of this information fresh in my mind and recorded on my template, I could close my eyes, breathe myself into an alpha state, and imagine the first scene.

LIVING RESEARCH

Do you know that historical fiction authors can take two or more years longer to write a book than anyone else due to the vast amount of research required? That's why many historical fiction authors choose a time and place they resonate with and hover there. History is vast, and if you add prehistory to that soup, you'll be swimming forever in different broths. But engaging in research is imperative and will stimulate your muses. Just be careful. You might turn into Alice and fall down a rabbit hole, in which case you might never write your book. Somewhere, you must stop researching and start writing the story.

The Dreaded Infodump

Be careful not to dump everything you've learned into the text just because you found it interesting. It's often noticeable as a change in narration. Suddenly, a new teacherly voice is telling you, the reader, something factual. A good editor will catch you "infodumping" and recommend you delete anything that's bogging down the story. Remember, you're painting a picture, not teaching history. This can happen to anyone, regardless of their writing experience. A writer friend mentioned a book recently where the author changed genres and smothered the story with historical facts. It's something we all struggle with.

Inspiration

Sometimes, one magazine article can jolt your muses into action. That's how *To Kill a King* emerged. I read a *National Geographic* article one night about two bog bodies that had been discovered in 2003 in the Irish midlands and couldn't let it go. One of the men was 6'6" tall. All that remains of him are his torso, arms, and hands with their manicured nails. Once I saw the photograph of his curled fingers, I was hooked.

Factor in that I have a borderline obsession with Ireland, and it doesn't take much to guess where that went. I needed to know him. Who was this enormous man? How did he end up ritually murdered and sunk in a bog? What was he like? Inside and out? Who did he love? Did he have a family? How could I give his life and death meaning?

I read everything I could find online. I even emailed Dr. Eamonn Kelly, who was the lead archaeologist at the Kingship and Sacrifice exhibit in the National Museum of Ireland. He studied Old Croghan Man (the name archaeologists gave to my man) and hypothesized the idea of sacred kingship, which involved a ritual marriage to the Goddess of the Land. As well, it's Dr. Kelly's theory that these kings were deposed and ritually murdered, as there is a sense of *overkill* in these cases. Dr. Kelly responded with answers to my questions. You'll find that most people you contact with legitimate research questions are helpful and glad to assist, especially if you share a passion for the subject.

In July 2017, I booked a room at Trinity College and flew to Dublin to research my bog man. I spent several days sitting beside his flattened, leathered torso in the museum exhibit. I photographed him every which way, along with anything else I could find from the height of the Celtic Iron Age. Old Croghan man's body was radiocarbon dated to 362-175 BCE. But what I really wanted from him was something personal. His name. What emerged at last was a deep, resonant sound like trilling r's. I called him Ruairí Mac Nia (pronounced *Rory*.)

I went to the local library in Dublin, got a temporary card, and pulled every research article I could find written by archaeologists about pagan Celtic Ireland. This involved filling out a form and waiting for the librarian to pull research material from the basement archives. The Druids were an oral culture that kept no written records and the Romans hadn't yet arrived in Britain, so most of what we know is based on the archaeological record. I sketched structures, maps, chariots, swords, musical instruments, and La Tene gold jewelry. At one point, when I was writing the book, I had to create a two-column chart comparing information from the archaeological record to things I'd intuited or imagined.

I rented a car and drove to ritual sites that would have been active around 200 BCE. Newgrange, in County Meath, has been in use for six thousand years. So has the hill of Uisneach (*Ish-neck*), which housed the "Stone of Divisions," the centerpiece between the four provinces. But there was one place left to go—Croghan Hill—where my man was inaugurated as king and then ritually murdered.

I picked up my daughter at Dublin airport, and we drove southwest. Croghan Hill is basically a cow pasture with a small village at its base. The bogland around it is being mined for peat, which is how my man's body was unearthed in 2003. We struggled to find our way. I had decent directions from a hillwalker site, but we couldn't find the right landmarks. Finally, we saw the community center and climbed the fence into the pasture, which, by the way, is home to a herd of curious cows.

I wanted to stand atop the hill and get a bird's-eye view. This gave me a feel for the landscape that surpassed Google Earth. I walked the same land where my man walked, and surveyed the distant hills, knowing that a fire would burn atop each during pagan festivals. To the west, I could see the hill of Uisneach, where Beltane is still celebrated every May 1. The striking black peat fields that surround the hill appear in both *To Kill a King* and *To Dance with Destiny*.

If you're curious, you can watch a video of me atop Croghan Hill on my Youtube channel.[1]

Cows, by the way, were so valued in ancient Ireland they were used as currency. They could even be used as an honor price to pay off a murder. So those cows, though they were a little scary when they trundled over to see us, were an essential feature of the prehistoric landscape.

---

1. https://www.youtube.com/@wlhawkin/videos

Finally, an image of Ruairí emerged.

He was clean-shaven, his nose long and straight, his cheekbones high and shadowed. His glittering amber eyes swept up at the corners, both amused and annoyed. The sides of his head were shaved close around his ears, but his copper hair was gelled up in eight-inch spikes that made him appear over seven feet tall. Mud and sweat were smeared across his chest. He was a huge man, broad, muscular, and naked save for a leather loincloth. *To Kill a King*

To put this in perspective with my intuitive process, I did all the research for this book in 2017, then came home and let it stew for almost two years. I even wrote another book during that time. I'm not sure if Estrada calls to me or if I call to him, but one day I knew it was time to write. I reread the research and began my meditative process. The scenes flew into place one after another as I asked the question, "What happens next?"

I Do Believe in Faeries

Sometimes the universe conspires to remind us that magic exists and there are spirit guides, angels, faeries, or whatever you care to call them, waiting to help you.

I suffer from multiple chemical sensitivities (MCS), and during my research trip to Ireland, I became quite ill due to exposure to scents and chemicals. I was traveling alone, which compounded my suffering. I'd stayed the first week at Trinity College in downtown Dublin.[1] I had a private bedroom, a shared bathroom across the hall, and a large lounge with cooking facilities. But at the height of summer, Dublin was awash in diesel fumes, cigarette smoke, perfumes, and aftershave, all of which triggered my nervous system.

---

1. https://www.visittrinity.ie/stay/

After seven days of research, I took the bus to the airport and picked up my rental car. From there, I drove to a Buddhist monastery in Co. Cavan,[2] which lies in the far north of the republic. It was lovely and green, and I slept with the windows wide open, so my symptoms eased. From Jampa Ling, I drove south to Uisneach[3] (the navel of Ireland.) After touring the site with Marty, an amazing storyteller, I drove on to Navan, and finally found my B&B. After four and a half hours of driving (in the left lane, seated on the right) I was exhausted.

The host was lovely and accommodating, but the house was awash with scented products. My nervous system spiked. I lay awake all night with the window open, taking Benadryl, terrified I was going to need an epipen. I remember getting up on my knees and leaning against the screen to suck in fresh air. My symptoms were so acute that I was considering going to the hospital, if I could sort out how to do that. Once my nervous system goes berserk, what a "normal" person might classify as a two, I feel like a twenty. I dozed off around five or six a.m. for maybe an hour. In the morning, I mentioned the problem to the host, but there wasn't much he could do. The chemicals from scented laundry detergents, fabric softeners, and plug-in air fresheners cannot be magically removed. So, I went off to explore the Hill of Tara, hoping to find some relief in the open country.

---

2. https://www.jampaling.org/

3. https://uisneach.ie/

Now, the Hill of Tara[4] is a sacred site rife with magic. It was the Royal Seat of 142 ancient High Kings of Ireland. It's an entrance to the Otherworld, and the Lia Fail, or Stone of Destiny, brought to Ériu by the Tuatha de Danann rests there. Beneath the faerie mounds are carved Neolithic stones with ancient symbols. Today, Tara is largely mounds and pasture lands, a dog-walker's dream, and it's still run like a farm, so you can walk the grassy vales for hours.

I wandered the fields, feeling horrible. My tongue was swollen and tingling and the antihistamines weren't helping at all. I was frightened. Alone. Lodged in a beta state. MCS creates brain fog, so I couldn't think straight. I was afraid to go back to the B&B, yet I was supposed to stay there again that night and the next. I breathed in the wind and sun, hoping it would magically cleanse me.

When I noticed a few people off in the far corner of a field, I approached and saw they were photographing a Faerie Tree. In Ireland, people tie ribbons on tree branches along with their prayers. I waited until I could be alone, then took the only scrap of fabric I had in my bag—a red lens cleaner—tied it to a branch, and made my appeal. *Please help me. I'm sick and alone, and I don't know what to do.*

On the way back to the B&B, as I passed a restaurant-motel called Tara House, a thought popped into my brain. *You don't have to stay there. You can leave. Stop here.* I turned the car around, went in, and inquired. I explained what was happening and asked if I could see the room, even smell it.

---

4. https://heritageireland.ie/places-to-visit/hill-of-tara/

"Certainly," the woman said. The room looked fine, but my heart sank. My highly sensitive nose could detect a musty odor, and on top of being sensitive to scents and chemicals, I'm allergic to dust and mold.

She noticed my disappointment and said, "Aww, you're suffering. Have you tried Josey's across the way?"

"Where?" I said. "Show me." And she did.

I walked across the road and met Josey out in her driveway. She had a room for two nights, which was exactly what I needed. We climbed the stairs, and she showed me a beautiful room fit for a princess. I felt like I was in a faerie tale. She understood about chemical sensitivity, assured me she didn't use any scented cleaners, and promised to cook me an Irish fry-up in the morning that was gluten and dairy-free. I teared up and told her she was my faerie godmother.

This is how quickly Spirit answers our call.

I went back to the B&B, packed up my things, and left a note to explain my departure. Then I drove to Josey's. She noticed the difference in me the next morning. I'd slept the night, and the swelling had gone down. That day, I was able to explore Newgrange and Knowth, two other places made sacred by the Faeries. So, remember, when you really need them, the Faeries will answer your call.

WORKING WITH ARTIFACTS

"The world is full of magic things, patiently waiting for our senses to grow sharper." W.B. Yeats

Working with Artifacts

Things have power. That's why we collect them. Why else would a bride want to wear "something old, something new, something borrowed, and something blue" on her wedding day? These four good-luck charms come from an Old English rhyme. Something old could be an heirloom that symbolizes family tradition. (I wore my aunt's white fur stole on my wedding day, as did my cousin.) Something new blesses a prosperous future. Something borrowed means you have trusted friends to whom you can turn in times of trouble. And blue, of course, is the color of loving spirit, peace, deep connection, clear skies, the watery unconscious, purity, and piety. Think of Mary's blue scarf.

Using Artifacts as Symbols

Tolkien[1] was the master of using artifacts as symbols. Remember the ring of power? What we can learn from him is how to weave an artifact so intensely into the story, it becomes a defining symbol that propels the action forward. You can either make a conscious decision to use an artifact in that way or the idea can come from your muses.

I wanted to use an artifact in *To Sleep with Stones* as I was working with an archaeologist, and it seemed like a good way in. After I read Lorraine Evan's work about Egyptians in Scotland,[2] I started my own research. When I saw an Egyptian broad collar, I was hooked. I decided that Sorcha would find the gold collar of Princess Meritaten (daughter of King Akhenaten and Queen Nefertiti) in the bottom of a Holy well in Kilmartin Glen, Scotland, and that discovery would impact the story. In a way, it acts as a MacGuffin—an object, event, or character in a film or story that serves to set and keep the plot in motion, though it's not usually important in and of itself.

Sometimes it's a conscious decision; other times, the artifact arrives in a dream or flash of insight. Recently, as I awoke in a dreamlike state, I saw one character pick up a bottle on a beach and another tease them, "What? Do you think a genie will appear?" That bottle will appear somewhere in my next book.

Using Artifacts for Characterization

Just like we have things we love that define us, so do our characters.

Michael Stryker has more artifacts than most, and they match his eccentric character traits. Michael is Estrada's best friend and lover. It took Estrada some time to realize he was bipolar. Some days he's Melancholy Michael; other days he's Manic Mandragora (his alter ego).

Michael fancies himself the reincarnation of Lord Byron. He's bisexual, charismatic, and a risk-taker—a moody, poetic, Byronic hero. He was even born on George Gordon's birthday, January 22nd, which makes him a Capricorn/Aquarius cusp. Michael chain-smokes and rolls his own cigarettes from the Turkish tobacco James Bond made famous. He has a silver monogrammed flip-top lighter (like my father used) and a gunmetal cigarette case. He imports both tobacco and papers. If you're intrigued by

Bond and his smoking habits, read this article in The James Bond Dossier.[3] Ian Fleming really knew how to brand a character.

Michael drinks fine wines (Chateau Margaux), snorts cocaine, smokes exceptional weed, and deals in "erotigens." He's the manager of a gothic nightclub in downtown Vancouver called Pegasus and enjoys spiking the shots with ecstasy (MDMA), which he calls "blood clots." His parties are legendary, and he's in great demand. His motto is: "It's just sex unless it's forced or bad, and then it's a travesty." This exotic libertine has a vampire fetish. He wears fangs and red contacts, black silk cloaks, and fine silk burgundy suits. He delights in beauty and eccentricity, quotes Byron's poetry, and truly believes he's "mad, bad, and dangerous to know." Lady Caroline Lamb[4] made that statement about Lord Byron after the publication of "Childe Harold" in 1812, and Michael has taken it to heart.

Michael's car is a 2001 BMW Z8 Roadster named "Crimson." She's blood red inside and out. He says the red interior cloaks his nocturnal vampire activities. It's actually a hand-me-down from his grandfather, and he adores her. He lives in a turreted flat in his grandfather's Queen Anne mansion. With its wraparound porch, railed balconies, and slanted roofs, the West Vancouver mansion has a distinctly Gothic feel.

---

3. https://www.thejamesbonddossier.com/lifestyle/smo king/james-bonds-cigarette-case.htm

4. The New York Times. April 1, 1989, Section 1, Page 26.

Estrada watched as Sensara took in the elegant silk draperies, burgundy leather couches, Michael's collection of imported hookahs, and the Persian carpets that ran rampant throughout the flat like so many opaline serpents. Like Byron, Michael had a penchant for the exotic. *To Charm a Killer*

Try This: Artifact as Muse

We did this as a group activity in our workshops, but you could also do it alone. Everyone chose an artifact and wrote about it. Amazingly, each person was drawn to something different. At the end of a designated time, we all shared aloud what we'd discovered. It was wonderful to hear where people took this and how beautiful and detailed the writing was.

Objectives:

- Enhance your ability to write from a sensory perspective

- Learn to spin a story from an object or artifact

Prepare:

First, gather some artifacts. You can even create an artifact box. Here are a few ideas: an old lock or key, special stones or crystals, a tree branch or flower, jewelry, a teacup, a silk scarf, a ring, a hat, a handkerchief, a drizzled candle or an antique candle holder, an old photograph, a fancy boot or high-heeled shoe, a jar of seeds, shells, or even a feather.

Sequence:

Choose an artifact from the box and engage in a multi-sensory experience. Close your eyes for a few moments, hold it in your hands, or hold your palms above it. Breathe with it. Meditate with it.

Then open your eyes and look. Really look. Describe it by size, shape, weight, and color.

Smell and taste if you dare.

Feel it. Turn it. Caress it. Hold it again in your hands. Can you feel its essence, its energy?

Put it to your ear. Does it make a sound? Does it speak? Do you hear a voice? Is it telling you a story? Do you see a person connected to it? Does a metaphor come to mind? Or is it symbolic in some way?

Close your eyes and go where it takes you.

Then put it down and write anything and everything without stopping or judging. Imbue it with emotions. Let the artifact tell you a story. All you have to do is write it down.

Extension:

Here are some topics to explore in your journal.

What do you own that symbolizes your identity? Are you connected to a color? A texture? A particular style? What things define you?

What artifacts or possessions do your characters need to make them unique and fully formed? Can you associate particular words or items with them? Without their stuff, who would they be?

ALLIES & ANIMALS

Many of us identify with a particular creature. It's not about physicality so much as symbolic essence and qualities. Though when you're in the zone with your spirit ally, you may take on its appearance and characteristics.

You might sit back right now, close your eyes, breathe, and ask yourself what animal you most identify with and why.

Thirty years ago, when I felt trapped in a relationship, what I longed for most was freedom. Our home bordered pastureland that was being developed into a golf course and estate homes. One of the horrors of this development was how it affected the hawks, who were losing their habitat. They'd fly madly into our windows, get stunned, and often die. I grew so passionate about the plight of the hawks that I wrote a piece which was published in *Common Ground*, Toronto.

Hawks symbolize freedom to me. The hawk is a magnificent bird whose power to see the world from afar and zero in on the smallest detail is legendary. When I took flight at last, I legally changed my name to signify my newfound freedom.

Hawkin means "kin of the hawks." By changing my name, I changed my identity and my world. This is the power of a spirit ally.

Susan Seddon Boulet[1] was an amazing artist who created mythical paintings of the spirit creatures she encountered while dreaming with her muse. Her layerings of skin, fur, feathers, and spirit affect us on a deeply psychological level. One of my best friends gave me a book of her paintings in 1996. *Shaman.* It was a transformative year for me, and the book has stayed with me through many flights. You can find Susan Seddon Boulet's paintings as prints and cards.

Finding Your Character's Spirit Ally

If you really want to flesh out your characters, find the spirit allies they blend with, and, as you write, this can merge into an extended metaphor. The animal ally becomes personified in the character.

My hero, Estrada, is a wolf. *El lobo.* He pads. He growls. He takes the shape of a sinewy black wolf in ritual. He's loyal to his pack. He'll thrust a man up against the wall and shake him like a wolf plays a rat. He uses knives like teeth and claws. When he takes a shamanic journey to rescue Michael's soul, Estrada's ally is a white wolf.

Others in Hollystone Coven are allied with spirit creatures too. Sensara is a black cobra. Daphne, an Earthy mama bear. Maggie's connection is with the horse. She gets a white and black Celtic warhorse tattooed on her arm, that you can

---

1. http://www.turningpointgallery.com/index.asp

view on the cover of *To Charm a Killer*. Maggie loves horses and is reborn through fire while saving the lives of a barn full of mares. Sorcha is a lioness who purrs and pounces. She's also described as a great ginger cat. Fearghas is an ox, and his stepbrother Bres, a weasel.

Giving your character animal traits brings definition, power, and cohesion to their character.

<hr>

A Celtic Shamanic Journey

In the next practice, you can take a shamanic journey to meet your own animal allies or those of your characters.

In the last several years, I've embraced the Celtic traditions of my father's family, the Carr clan. The bulk of my ancestors are Celts, and I feel particularly at home in Ireland. It may be an ancestral memory or remembrance of a past life that calls me there. I don't know. But the lure is as strong as that used by Finn McCool to hook the Salmon of Knowledge.

I journey often to the Underworld. On a recent journey, I was met at the entrance by a beautiful black horse. I've loved horses all my life and used to ride bareback and bare-legged in the summer. After greeting the horse, I led it to a rock and mounted it. As I rode through the landscape, the sensations were intensely physical. I could feel its warm hair against my bare skin and used my legs to guide it like I did as a child. There was no bridle or bit. This horse was wild and free, yet took me where I needed to go because our minds and spirits linked. The horse is one of my spirit allies.

How to use a Shamanic Journey in your Writing

When you're writing with your muse, you blend with your characters, meaning you journey with them. This lends authenticity to the writing.

I studied Druidry with The Order of Bards, Ovates, and Druids[2] for a few years and still practice these techniques. Also, I used some of the work of an Oregon woman. In *By Oak, Ash & Thorn: Modern Celtic Shamanism*, D. J. Conway uses Druid concepts. Her guided visualizations and explanations of the Otherworlds are inspiring and helpful. As with any book, take what you need and leave the rest. The journey that follows is an adaptation of Conway's work that I've incorporated into my practice.

In *To Render a Raven*, when Michael Stryker becomes catatonic, Estrada takes a shamanic journey into the Underworld to retrieve his shattered soul. Estrada's one-year-old daughter has been kidnapped, and Michael has information Estrada needs to find her. Magus Dubh (pronounced *Dove*), a Druid priest from Glasgow suggests the journey and acts like a guide for Estrada. When it came

---

2. https://druidry.org/

time to write Estrada's underworld journey, I set out along with him.

To prepare, I cued up Tim Norton's *Traditional Shamanic Drum Journey* on my phone. You can find a free version on YouTube.[3] If you have a drum or rattle, you can create your own beats. I prefer to lie flat in corpse position, so I use a soundtrack. I'd carved out a good thirty minutes in which to travel and another hour following to write about our experience. What occurred was amazing. You can read the complete journey in *To Render a Raven: Underworld*.

If you're writing a shamanic scene, you can change the verb tense from past to present just for that scene. This makes it more immediate and mystical. Changing tenses or points-of-view signals the reader to pay attention. Here's an excerpt:

"Walk down," Dubh says.

Estrada obeys. Each footfall is a descent into darkness, and then a torch flares in the smooth golden wood of the tree. Light. A sign of hope and promise. Inspired, he quickens his pace, skipping down the spiral stairs, sinking deeper into the tree where the rich wood scent fills his senses. At last, he comes to a circular door, shoves it open and steps out.

"Michael? Where are you, Michael?"

Estrada runs barefoot across the cold damp sand until

---

3. https://youtu.be/jeSZzaUod-w

he meets a river. It's not very wide, he decides. Perhaps a mile. Above, the sky is a violet haze studded with stars, the full orb of the moon reflecting in the dark water. In the distance, he sees the river cascading from a snow-capped mountain. Swirling over jagged rocks, it forms a natural barrier across the land. But here, the water is still.

Tiny ripples erupt, created by the lips of fish. A sudden splash here, a metallic flash there, reveal the presence of life beneath. But what life lives in the Underworld? Lovecraft's Dagon? Or worse? Dare he try to swim across? There's no bridge.

Celtic Otherworlds

On your next practice, you'll take a guided shamanic journey. But first, here are a few simplified notes on the terrain of the Celtic Otherworlds. There are many ways to travel. I'm taking you the way I've traveled successfully. It's a simplified route, and I'm by no means an expert. This is a journey similar to other visual journeys we've taken already, but it's colored by a more specific mythology.

The Spiral Stair

In this landscape, we find three worlds or sacred spaces of consciousness connected by a central pole—the Upperworld, Middleworld, and Underworld. On our journey, we'll enter through a large tree, the Celtic Tree of Life. I find the simplest visual is of a spiral staircase with a doorway/portal and landing in the center. The Middleworld refers to the world we know and frequent, and it's from here we venture forth and return. When you travel, you simply walk up or down the stairs.

You can never be trapped in the Otherworlds. You're always in control, and you can return at any time by simply becoming conscious of your body.

The Underworld can be reached by descending a staircase counter-clockwise (walking to your left). Let's be clear. The Celtic Underworld is nothing like the Christian hell. It's a pleasant place where souls await rebirth, as the Celts believed in reincarnation. It's also the abode of faeries who live underground in the sidhe (*shee*) the mounded prehistoric tombs of Ireland. An enchanting land, the Underworld is inhabited by gods, goddesses, and a variety of animals, plants, stones, and mythical creatures who can communicate. It's here we'll go to meet our spirit ally.

Above is the Upperworld, a place of enlightenment and the abode of immortals, advanced souls, and deities. There are also animals, sentient beings, and mythical creatures in the Upperworld. To reach there, you would ascend the staircase by walking clockwise. I've yet to travel there.

Anecdote: The Blue Butterfly

A few years ago, when I was contemplating a life change, I took a personal shamanic journey.

In meditation, I cross the stone bridge, bundle my problems, and toss them into the river to watch them sink.

Then I walk along a stream that leads to a waterfall. On the right is the giant willow, where I like to sleep. On the left is a tall elm from childhood that reaches into the clouds. I walk through a waterfall into a cave lit with honeyed candles. Picking up a torch, I follow a pathway down, down, down. The door opens into a green field full of blue butterflies. One of them comes to sit on my arm and returns with me. An ally.

Later, I analyzed the blue butterfly from an intellectual perspective. I discovered that it symbolizes grace, freedom from self-imposed restrictions, transformation to a new state, and the final stage of a metamorphosis. That seemed logical and  fit with my current dilemma, which was trying to decide on the next phase of my career.

Two weeks later, I was working again with the blue butterfly. During meditation I heard: *You are the blue butterfly. Be free and know you are loved and protected. You are the blue butterfly on your journeys when you travel to the lower world, under the earth. That's where you freed that part of yourself. It's not just an ally. It's you. A shattered part of your soul that fled long ago because it couldn't live in the sadness. Now it's returned. Go to the oak tree. You hide in the arms of the willow, but it's time to cling to the oak. Feel its skin against your skin. Climb into its branches. It's the path to the Upperworld.*

There's a difference between analytical thought and intuitive knowledge. Yes, the blue butterfly did symbolize freedom and transformation but there was more. I trusted in my guides and walked into my new career feeling more whole, confident, and energized.

Try This: Celtic Shamanic Journey

Try taking this shamanic journey to connect with your spirit ally and/or conjure your character's ally.

Objective:

- Experience a shamanic journey

- Meet your spirit ally/animal

Preparation:

You might want to use an audio drum track to transform the soundscape. I use a "Traditional Shamanic Drum Journey" created by Tim Norton. There are three journeys on this album, and all will move you quickly into the theta state. Earphones enhance the experience, and your neighbors will appreciate your consideration. Also, when the music changes it's a signal that it's time to retrace your steps and climb back up the spiral staircase and into the ordinary world.

Cue up your laptop or gather your notebook and pen before you begin. I suggest you record the following journey as an audio track beforehand or for a deeper experience, record the journey with the drumming track playing in the background. That way, you don't have to read and remember. You can just sink into the experience. Silence your technology and find a warm, comfortable position where you can fully relax, knowing you'll be traveling in an altered state of consciousness for the next twenty to thirty minutes.

At the conclusion of this practice, your task is to write about your experience. Who or what is your spirit ally/animal? Describe it using all your senses. How does this creature affect you? How do you affect it? How does it reveal itself in your life? How can your spirit ally/animal be present in your writing?

As an option, you could send your character on this shamanic journey and travel along with them, or you could do this journey on behalf of your character.

Sequence:

First, relax your physical body by taking several deep breaths. Then begin a deep relaxation from toes to crown by using this Druid light body exercise:

Imagine the bright, warm rays of the sun caressing the bottoms of your bare feet. As you do this, your feet begin to feel warm. Allow the light to float up from your feet and penetrate each bone, joint, muscle, tendon, and cell in warm golden rays. Slowly, the light travels up your legs and through the chakra at the base of your spine. It follows the curve of your spine, touching the sacral chakra in your belly, and the power chakra in your solar plexus, along with all your internal organs. The light floods your heart and spins down your shoulders and arms into the palms of your hands.

A gentle golden warmth spreads throughout your body as all cells are nourished by this healing, expanding energy. From your heart, the light travels upward, bathing the throat chakra and every curve and organ in your face, then moves through your brain and third eye. Following the beat of the drums and rattle, the light moves through the top of your head and bathes your crown chakra, then flows into the astral bodies that surround your physical body and out into your aura. You feel yourself expand with the light.

Fully cleansed and exhilarated, you find yourself in a forest clearing. Hearing the murmur of water, you follow the sound to an old stone bridge that arches over a river. You walk halfway across the bridge and stop, feeling the cool, mossy stone of the bridge with your hands. Gazing over into the still water below, you realize you're about to enter a sacred land—a land that cannot be entered when you're carrying any problems or worries.

Finding a pale linen sack lying on the ledge of the bridge, you open it wide, take a deep breath, and exhale all your worries, concerns, and fears into the linen sack. It's like blowing up a balloon. Hold the end tightly and tie it off with a cord, then cast it over the side of the bridge into the dark waters below. You know the Mother Earth will absorb it, and all will be well.

Feeling lighter, you continue across the bridge and follow a woodland path up into a forest. At the top of the rise, is an enormous oak tree. It's incredible. Older than time, like *Yggdrasil* (Igdrasill), the ancient Norse tree that connects the cosmos, or *Crann Bethadh* (Cran Baha), the Celtic Tree of Life. You know that this special tree connects the Underworld and the Upperworld. You know that you're about to leave the Middleworld and travel down into the Underworld.

As you lay your hand on the bark of the oak, you feel its beautiful energy beating like the heart of the drum. A door opens beneath your hand, and you see that inside is a landing. A spiral staircase runs through the tree. To your left, it curves upwards, and to your right, it curves down. You turn to the right and begin to follow the carved steps down inside the tree. It's dark, but honeyed candles glow from niches set into the walls of the tree and allow you to find your footing. You continue to step down counter-clockwise, following the slight curve of the winding staircase. At the bottom, you come to another door. You take a breath, exhale, and open it.

Take in the scene in front of you. The Underworld is a safe and welcoming place, and you know you can walk here without fear. Time has stopped and is of no importance. You step out and know you will remember everything you see, hear, feel, and encounter. Every tree, flower, animal, and insect. Every experience.

One creature shows itself in such a way that you know it's the spirit ally you were meant to meet. It may give you a message in some way. Take it in, and remember.

When the drumbeat changes, it's time to return. Wherever you are, retrace your steps back to the doorway and climb the staircase to the landing in the Middle World. From there, you can follow the forest path back to the arched stone bridge and return to your body.

Slowly begin to feel sensations in your body, and when you are sufficiently back, pick up your pen or open your laptop and record your journey.

⸻◆⸻

Anecdote: The Linen Sack

Many people suffer from anxiety. Often, we experience physical symptoms. When I'm really stressed, I feel tension in my neck and throat. The constriction makes breathing and swallowing difficult. At its worst, my larynx spasms, and I can't take a breath or swallow. If you've ever experienced having the wind knocked out of you, you know how terrifying it feels. Here's something that helps me.

Walking in nature relaxes me. One day, when my neck and throat were particularly tight and uncomfortable, I decided to do physically what I do in my shamanic journey. Standing atop a bridge, I gazed down into the water below. Picking up an imaginary linen sack, I opened it wide, took a deep breath, then held it tightly to my pursed lips and blew my worries into the sack in a long, slow exhale. No one was around, and it felt so good, I did it twice more. With three big breaths in the sack, I tied it off and cast it over the bridge into the water.

My muscles immediately relaxed and I heard a voice say, *"Yes, you can make your muscles tight and you can also release them."*

Later, when I saw a speech-language pathologist for my laryngeal spasms, the first exercise she taught me was blowing through a plastic tube into a bottle of water. The action of exhaling through pursed lips physically releases and relaxes the muscles in your throat and neck.

"Wow," I said. "I do this when I'm out walking." She was curious, so I explained how I blew into the imaginary linen sack. She told me to keep it up.

Intuitively, I'd found a way to control my anxiety that worked. Now, when I'm out in the world and feel anxious, I take a few moments to close my eyes and imagine myself on the bridge. I purse my lips and exhale my worries into the linen sack. It's a quick fix that brings immediate relief. You can do this physically or through a meditation journey. Both will bring relief.

ARCHETYPES & THE HERO'S JOURNEY

Plato

To understand archetypes, we must return to one of the Greek philosophers. Plato. This gifted soul, who lived in Athens between 428 BC and 348 BCE, understood that reality exists beyond the physical. We may interact with the physical realm as we go about our lives, but it's only a shadow of the spiritual realm, or what he called "The Realm of Forms."

The Forms are perfect, abstract ideals that transcend time and space. Justice is a Form. Beauty is a Form. Good is a Form. Though the physical form may be imperfect, it originates from a spiritual essence that is always perfect.

The Greek word *arche* means origin or source. So, in Plato's vision, the Archetype was the source or type for everything that existed in the physical world—its Form.

Carl Gustav Jung

In the early 1900s, Swiss psychiatrist and psychologist Carl Jung developed several concepts we're familiar with in contemporary culture: the idea of extraverted and introverted personality types, the Collective Unconscious, and archetypes. Jung believed that there is a place of shared experience that each of us can access through our mind. At first, he called these forms primordial images, then archetypes. These patterns (or Forms) within the Collective Unconscious are universal in nature, can be expressed through behavior and images, and can be tweaked to fit cultures. We inherit them. We don't have to study them or reach out to them, as they're already a part of our psyche. There are archetypal events, figures, and motifs. Through dreams and fantasies, we explore and experience the archetypes of the Collective Unconscious. And as writers, they are our best friends.

Joseph Campbell

Jung noted, as did comparative mythologist Joseph Campbell, that there are timeless motifs and archetypes that repeat in cultures around the world. Campbell expanded on Jung's work when he wrote his book, *The Hero with a Thousand Faces*. His theory on the Hero's Journey illustrates the ultimate narrative archetype, and within it are embedded other common archetypes. Why are they so recognizable? Because they exist in the realm of the Collective Unconscious, we access them in our dreams. Storytellers throughout time have delivered them to us through myths, folktales, and fairy tales.

Not long ago, comparatively speaking, George Lucas brought us The Hero's Journey in his first Star Wars movie. After familiarizing himself with Joseph Campbell's work, Lucas set out to create an archetypal film. Since then, several screenwriters, producers, and novelists have worked with this amazing structure and knowledge, including me.

THE ARCHETYPAL HERO'S JOURNEY

Act One

I resonate with the Hero's Journey so emphatically that I can plot my story on the circle after I write the first draft. I also teach it in a workshop—which I offer here in a condensed form—that highlights the embedded archetypes in a three-act structure used by screenwriters. For a wonderfully detailed study of how to plot your novel or screenplay, see *The Writer's Journey: Mythic Structure for Writers* by Chris Vogler.[1] There are several editions. Vogler's work fits beautifully into my writing process and always inspires me. Often, just reading it will trigger a story.

The Hero (not gender-specific) is an archetype. The Hero is someone who follows a vision greater than themselves.

---

1. Vogler, Chris. The Writers Journey: Mythic Structure for Writers. Michael Wiese Productions: California, 1998

Frequently, something has been taken from them or something is missing (they have an internal problem), and their quest is to find and recover it. They're often orphaned and have a tragic flaw. Still, they're prepared to sacrifice their time and even their lives to save something or someone. At the end of the journey, they recover what they've lost or discover some new elixir to help mankind. The Hero must leave their Ordinary World/Reality to make the journey. Below is a diagram I created for a workshop. You can find it on Prezi.[2]

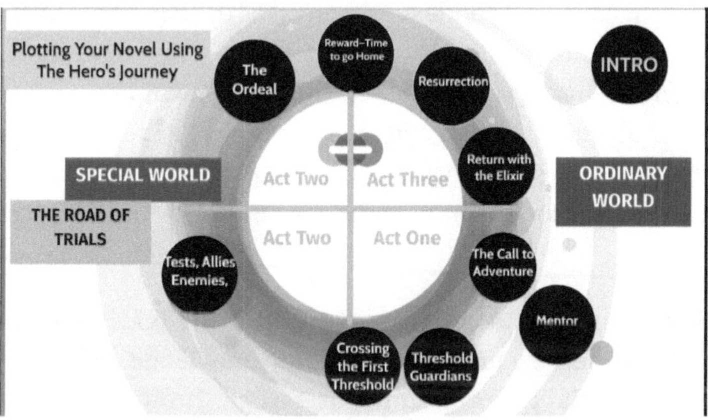

Frequently, the Hero is called to their adventure by **The Herald.** The Greek god Hermes was the messenger of the gods. The Herald often inspires a shift by offering an invitation or challenge to the hero called **The Call to Adventure.** This might take the form of a letter, a phone call or text, a dream or supernatural visit, the loss of a loved one, a kidnapping, a fixated idea in the mind of the Hero, or even a piece of music.

---

2. https://prezi.com/p/v_k4w1ac-xps/the-heros-journey/

Try to create new and exciting ways to express the archetypes in your writing. In *To Charm a Killer*, the sound of Dylan's bagpipes in the woods reaches Maggie and her dog, and they follow the music to where the coven is conducting a ritual.

Often, The Hero tries to deny or reject The Call, but once they accept, they're usually offered aid by **Mentor.** Remember our friend Odysseus from chapter one? He is King of Ithaca, but after the Trojan War, he's held captive by Calypso and can't return home to his wife Penelope and son Telemachus. The goddess Athena takes the guise of Mentor, who is an old family friend and guardian of Telemachus. As Mentor, she appears to Telemachus and encourages him to fight off the hordes of suitors all living off Penelope while vying to marry her. Athena also persuades Telemachus to take a ship and go on a journey to search for his long-lost father.

The Mentor is usually wise and in some way trains or aids the hero by providing wisdom, knowledge, skills, and often special gifts that must be earned through learning, sacrifice, and commitment to the task. Western culture has made a business model out of the mentor archetype. You can receive mentoring or be mentored. A good mentor will support you in reaching your goals but stay out of your way, so the journey is your own. Both Gandalf and Dumbledore are mentors you may recognize.

Threshold Guardians. As the hero attempts to cross the threshold into the Special World, he or she often encounters archetypal forces that try to thwart their passage. They might issue threats or warnings. Sometimes, the villain sends his thugs to taunt or even try to kill the hero. Their role is to illustrate the danger looming in the special world. The special world is a dynamic contrast to the ordinary world the hero has left behind. Think Kansas and Oz.

Act Two

On the **Road of Trials**, the hero will face all manner of allies and enemies who will test their courage and worthiness. Each will help raise the stakes. Some will be benevolent, while others will be deadly. Here are a few archetypes that occur frequently in popular culture:

- Addict: common in contemporary stories, the addict is willing to risk everything to get what they need

- Artist: embodies a passion to create

- Athlete: someone who strives for physical excellence, often in sport

- Bully: a coward who lashes out to make themselves feel more powerful

- The Child: symbolizes light and innocence, unless it's a Shadow Child. Then the child may take the hero for a ride on the dark side.

- Clown: the funny character that always tries to lighten things up. Sometimes the hero's sidekick is a clown to contrast the serious demeanor of the hero. Usually, it's a mask or a role play.

- Detective: some heroes are detectives; other heroes work with detectives; some must battle detectives, police, or military antagonists. Clever and intuitive, they're though not always honest.

- Femme Fatale: Beware this creature. She will enchant you, spin a web around you, and eat you for supper. This does not need to be a woman, though the energy is usually sexy and feminine. Think about Glenn Close's character in *Fatal Attraction*.

- Gods and Goddesses: Two of my characters are Celtic gods, and my Wicca priestess has channeled the goddess on occasion. Power and magic defines this archetype.

- Healer: likely will be needed by the hero at some point when things heat up. Both physical and emotional wounds need healing.

- Hedonist: someone who shows an insatiable appetite for pleasurable activities (sex, good wine, good food, and parties). Estrada's lover, Michael Stryker, is a hedonist.

- Judge: the judge may dispense positive or negative justice depending on their own experiences and agenda.

- King and/or Queen: the royals have power, want to keep it, and want to gain more

- Knight: the true knight symbolizes chivalry, honor,

and self-sacrifice, especially when it involves rescuing someone in danger from something truly evil. He's often a male romantic figure.

- Lover: heroes often meet a lover in the Special World. Sometimes these two team up. Often, the lover is a pawn in the villain's game.

- Poet: a creative soul who searches for truth and beauty

- Princess: a beautiful, often powerless daughter in need of rescue

- Prince: sometimes a hero and sometimes a villain, the prince usually wants to become something else—the king.

- Rebel: where there's a power regime, there's a rebel. Western culture romanticizes rebels, so our heroes often organize or join rebel forces.

- Saboteur: someone who presents themselves as helpful but intends to thwart the hero's progress.

- Shapeshifter: someone who can change in appearance or transform physically into another creature

- Slave: powerless, impoverished, and needing freedom

- Thief: foxy, sneaky, not to be trusted unless what's being stolen needs stealing

- Trickster: the tricks of the trickster often inspire growth but sometimes just wreak havoc. The Trickster can be a comic character, a riddler, a magician, or a wizard.

- Vampire: someone who drains power for their own pleasure and gain

- Villain: the villain locks horns with the hero. These two must have equitable power and skill to make it interesting. It's important, therefore, to humanize the villain in some way. No one is born evil. Don't just show us how evil the villain is; show us why.

- Virgin: symbolizes purity and innocence

This is just a partial list of possibilities. Remember to avoid clichés. Strive for something new and turn these archetypes on their heads.

Act Two begins with the **Threshold Crossing** and is twice as long as Act One. This is the meat of the journey, where your muse can run wild. How do you keep the reader engaged? Raise the stakes. Every test should be harder. Every injury is worse than the last. Every emotional blow cuts that much deeper. And then, they finally reach. . .

The Ordeal: a place where the hero must face the death of something that will transform them (their greatest fear, loss, change, or even their own physical death). It's intense. You must keep your reader riveted and cheering for the hero to survive. Often, the hero fights the villain and appears to die here. Perhaps another character witnesses the hero's apparent death. There is a moment when we think they're doomed. And then the hero is reborn, changed, and transformed so they can claim the reward, whatever that might be (discovery, epiphany, promotion, initiation, that which was lost is found, lovers are reunited). Finally, they get to go home.

Act Three

But home doesn't always come easy. In fact, it takes a whole third act the size of Act One to bring the hero home. Sometimes heroes don't want to go home, or the villain calls in reinforcements, or the hero discovers there's a supervillain a step above who has yet to be dispatched.

The Resurrection is the climax of Act Three. It's usually a battle between good and evil, which the hero must fight alone. In an epic, if the hero doesn't win this battle, the villain will destroy the world. This is where we see duels, shoot-outs, emotional confrontation, a shift in consciousness, or some sort of sacrifice. Perhaps the hero gives up the treasure, loses someone they love, or offers themselves as the sacrifice. In the end, the hero returns to the Ordinary World with ...

The Elixir, is an archetype unto itself. The elixir is something powerful to share with humanity. Some common elixirs are social change, experience, knowledge or power, fortune or wealth, good health, or justice.

Whatever has occurred, the hero is changed within and without.

ANTIDOTE TO FEAR: NO SALES

NO ONE WILL BUY MY BOOK.

This is a very real fear that hobbles writers and potential sales.

Ask yourself: Why am I writing this book? Is it to sell or because writing it will give me joy? Some of us hope for both but each writer is unique.

Maybe you're enthused about creating a memoir based on your life or someone important to you. Many writers, including myself, are researching and recording family history. We want to take our findings and give them form. Some writers are looking back on their own life and writing snippets of creative non-fiction. If this is something you want to try, I offer a chapter on "Writing Memoir with your Muse." Others are compiling favorite recipes into cookbooks or a lifetime of poetry into a volume of reflections. Still others are trying their hand at writing fiction, nonfiction, or screenplays. Because Indie publishing is relatively simple now, anything you envision you can create and offer for sale.

If you write to nurture yourself and your creative spirit, you'll be successful no matter how many books you sell. It's hard not to compare yourself to others, but in doing so, you risk losing the magic. We're bombarded daily with other writer's successes and FOMO (Fear of Missing Out) is as deadly an enemy as "writing to sell" can be. Writing what you think the market wants isn't just a gamble, it's hobbling. Remember, thinking pulls us out of theta-brain and away from our muses. And the market is an ever-changing enigma. That's why an author might sell one, two, or even three books to a publisher and then spend years trying to find an agent or editor to accept their next piece. Some writers become so discouraged, they give up writing.

It doesn't matter if your book sells or not. What matters is that you can still feel the magic because what you feel, you create. When your readers feel the magic, they will come back for more. And trust me, there will be readers.

TRY THIS: CONSTRUCTING CABINS, CASTLES & CAVERNS

We find ourselves in our writing, and if we're lucky, we also lose ourselves.

You don't have to be an architect to design Hogwarts or a Death Star, to build a contemporary estate, a haunted house, or a cozy cabin for your characters, or to take them spelunking through wild caves.

You can scan images, digest the lay of the land and snap photographs, trigger your imagination by watching films, and visit brick-and-mortar locations to feel the energy. Remember that all dwellings hold the vibrations created by people and events. That's why it's important to smudge your home with sage regularly, especially if you've just moved into a new residence or you're traveling between hotel rooms.

Moreover, stored within our brain is a lifetime of episodic events from which we can recreate rich sensory experiences.

Recalling Memories

Memories are stored in the medial temporal lobes, notably the hippocampus and parietal and prefrontal cortices. During memory recall, the visual cortex becomes as active as it was when we first experienced the episode. Like a story, an episode involves details like who, when, what, and where. Using episodic memory, we can time-travel to landscapes and structures we determine are important enough to store. Late childhood seems to be a key time for memories to stick, as our brains are sufficiently developed and our lives are filled with emotional experiences that are memory paste. Episodes are dependent on feelings. The more meaningful and intense the moment, the more we recall.

This is a practice you can adapt to any genre.

Objectives:

- Tune into your long-term memory to recall images and sensory descriptions

- Sharpen your observation skills

- Turn those descriptions into settings

Sequence:

With your writing materials at hand, close your eyes and take a few deep breaths. Feel yourself moving from beta brain into alpha brain, where you are relaxed and situated in the present moment. From here, we're going to take a walk into the past. Some of us do not come from safe spaces, so choose a place in which you feel comfortable. If you'd rather not go yourself, send your character. This could be a home you lived in as a child, a cabin you remember, or even a castle you visited that left an impression.

Find yourself in front of a door. Look carefully at the material and the design. Is there a window, a knob, or a latch? Push the door open and step inside. There's no one here but you, and it's a completely safe space. As you explore, be aware of any energy you feel.

As you begin to walk through this dwelling, take notes from floor to ceiling and wall to wall. Notice the colors, the furnishings, any odors that arise, the visual details, or sounds you might hear. Specific places may draw your attention. Just observe and let them go. Follow your feet down hallways and into rooms. Look for knickknacks, art, dishes, plants, the age and condition of furniture, quilts or throws, perhaps a piano or other musical instruments, or a hearth filled with photographs. Look at the windowpanes and at that layer of dust or polish on wooden surfaces. Try to determine the season. Has Jack Frost painted designs on the windows? Are there decorations? Is a fan blowing the curtains?

If you find your bedroom and feel comfortable, enter and have a look around. What strikes you in this room where you slept as a child?

If you're comfortable, check out the less familiar rooms, perhaps the attic or cellar.

When you feel you've seen and explored enough, come back to the present moment, pick up your pen, and write about your experience. Capture as much detail as possible.

Your Next Task: Take It Further

Your next task is to build a dwelling with your words, something that fits the atmosphere of the piece you're writing. Remember, the story itself is about people, and the setting is the backdrop. So, you need to add characters to elicit emotion from your reader. In some fiction, the house becomes a character. Think of it as a living, breathing entity. How does that change things?

If you're writing a memoir, you've done all the research already. You just need to spend quiet time with your memories and find the right words to capture them on the page.

If you're writing fiction, you've got a blank canvas. You need to know your timeframe and the motivations of your characters and work from there. When in doubt—which happens when you're in beta brain and trying to think—sit, breathe, and ask: "Where are we? Tell me about this place. Tell me what happens here."

One of the things I love about being an author is the ability to create settings that fit the characters and plot. You'll never get bored as a writer.

How I Use This Technique to Write Urban Fantasy

Envisioning a dwelling is integral to setting a scene, but remember, stories are all about people. The Taylor home on Hawk's Claw Lane features in my mysteries. In the first book, Maggie Taylor explains how her father built it from logs. At the end of that book, Maggie and her mother move to Ireland and rent it to Sensara, Daphne, and Raine, so it becomes the Hollystone Coven headquarters. They even keep Maggie's black Labrador retriever, Remington Steele.

Estrada's daughter is born there in a birthing pool on the back deck. They celebrated Lucy's first birthday there. I know that home intimately. Two girls are abducted from the upstairs bedroom in that house. It's real enough for me to wander around inside at night.

In *To Render a Raven*, I created a Spanish vampire's palace in The Broughton Islands that resembles the Alhambra. As I've never been to Spain, I assembled the energy and architecture from photographs and then renovated them to suit the forested islands of British Columbia.

Estrada pushed open the mahogany double doors, and they stepped through. The deep scarlet walls were tiled, like the floor, in flamboyant waves of terra cotta, ivory, and sapphire. Three tall pine trees grew from the earth, their tops reaching toward a glass coffered ceiling. All

was quiet, though bodies swayed in woven hammocks from the branches or lazed in piles on Persian rugs and red-gold damask pillows. An arm or leg dangled. Vampires passing the day, and not a coffin to be seen.

Let's kill them as they sleep, Dubh thought, raising his staff.

But Estrada touched a finger to his lips to signal silence and ventured into the nest. The others followed. The furniture, brightly patterned couches and chaises, pillows, and ottomans, were scattered around tropical plants in a horseshoe shape. Honeyed candles cast an eerie glow against the carmine walls. The room reeked of wax and wine, foul flesh, and something indefinable.
To Render a Raven

How I Use This Technique to Write a Historical Novel

The Iron Age hill fort in *To Kill a King* sits atop a 768-foot volcano. I physically stood atop the hill, but no hill fort exists now, so I had to create it from research sketches and my imagination. The fort is constructed of wooden posts, sharpened like palisades. Inside the gates, the wattle and daub dwellings are large and round. People cluster around a central hearth, eat from trenchers, and sleep close enough to each other to be aware of all nocturnal activities (sounds, and yes, smells).

In one of the scenes, I featured the volcanic cavern that lies below them. I haven't rappelled inside a volcano, but some people have *with cameras*. I watched enough video to get a feel for it, and then I set my characters free and let them find their way.

How I Use This Technique to Write Memoir

I remember the details of my childhood home accurately. That's not surprising since I spent the first sixteen years of my life living there, and things were slow to change. If I stand on the gravel road in front of our house, I recall it vividly: the crunch of rubber tires on gravel; the white frame bungalow and blue cement steps. As I walk up the drive to the back, I recall cracked pavement heaped with ant hills (I collected ants in jars); a red latched screen door; elegant willows and rippling Manitoba maples; two wells; a broken gate; and several flowerbeds. In fact, I can recall the trees and plants, their colors, and their species in the greatest detail as I spent most of my time outdoors alone, romping, riding, or swinging by my knees from a makeshift trapeze (a metal pipe) in the apple tree near my playhouse (a packing crate with a peaked roof) with an outhouse behind it.

Creative Nonfiction

One of today's trendy genres is creative nonfiction and memoir is a branch of it. In essence, writers reveal shards of truth using creative writing techniques. There are few rules—the most basic one being to tell the truth—so there's room for experimentation. I wrote the following piece for a recent university writing course. You'll notice that I switch narrators and tenses often. The child's story is told in the present tense to create a sense of immediacy, but it's touched by the adult's commentary. In this particular assignment, the topic was place, and the prompt suggested I write at the intersection of history and the environment. I recommend you try this technique. You never know what memories you might unearth.

Haven

The cow field east of our barn is bursting with honey bees who dart between the daisies. Not those dainty English daisies, but the ornery oxeye, *leucanthemum vulgare*, named after a working bullock, the commoner of cows. I have a steer of my own—a Hereford-Holstein cross—and feel his docile strength when I climb on his back. I've just turned eight and wear this place like a pair of wings. Plucking a daisy, I tuck it into my light brown hair. Later, my friend will weave me a crown of daisies to wear to my wedding.

Orange monarch butterflies, like fluttering stained-glass windows, catch the June breeze and follow me as I meander through the soft, green grass in my bare feet. Each spring, I capture some of their chubby black and yellow-striped larvae on their milkweed stalks and set them up in mason jars. They ravage the leaves until they're fat enough to spin turquoise chrysalids edged in gold. When they crack from their crystal shells and emerge to stretch their damp, sticky wings, I release them to fly south for the winter.

I am the ragtag nymph of the woods, and this is my haven.

We are in need of such things. Havens. In school, we're warned about the Cold War. Regular people are building bomb shelters, even here in southern Ontario. The Russians have just placed nuclear missiles in Cuba, an island on our side of the sea, and, though I love President Kennedy, I'm not sure he can convince Mr. Khrushchev not to push the button. But one thing I know: if The End happens, I'd rather be here in my haven than locked in an airless underground cement bunker lined with tin cans. I can't imagine opening a door to a blackened hellish world—a bleak, choking bonfire that stretches endlessly into oblivion. I'd rather evanesce to heaven, here and now.

As I scramble down the small hill that leads to the stream, I catch a glimpse of a dark brown, pointed head. My muskrat is a loner like me. I've never smelled the telltale male musk, so assume she's female. I never found her lodge. She must have tunneled along the stream to a secret haven of her own. I'm shocked to discover that most muskrats don't survive longer than two years. I'm lucky to have known her then.

Green frogs peek from short grasses along the stream. Their throaty croaks, like the thwacks of fat elastic bands, halt as I approach. I gulp the fresh, earthy air and squat by the stream to dip my hands. Though I'm not supposed to, I cup them and sip the sweet, coppery water. Water bugs and minnows dart through the slow, singing stream, along with invisible amoebic creatures that can make me sick. I see broken willows and tiny hoof prints, even tan scruff caught in the crotches where deer have come to browse. Last year, a lost pony named

Puddles joined the herd of wild deer in our pasture, and when we returned him to Stoney Creek Riding Stables, the grateful owner offered me English riding lessons. Soon, I'll have a horse of my own, and this will be a haven for us all.

Elm lives just on the other side of the rusty fence in the neighbor's field, and is so broad I can't get my arms all the way around her. I love the feel of her crusty gray bark against my cheek. Her trunk is tall, but I use the rickety, square-paned metal fence as my boost. I can just reach her lowest branch from the top, lock both hands around her, and swing my legs up like I do on my makeshift trapeze.

Elm is the queen of my haven. Her canopy reaches to the clouds and stretches over all the shrubs of the hedgerow. Her dark green leaves have veins and teeth. I remember the smell, like rich burnt paper, as I ironed autumn leaves between wax sheets for my annual collection. I climb as high as I dare, sink back into her comforting arms, and survey my kingdom. I could stay here forever, and later, when I practice Druidry, this is where I come in my visions.

No one can see me in my haven, and I never bring anyone here. Not even Lillian, my summer friend, whose family lives in Toronto and owns a cottage just five minutes walk north. So I can't fathom how it happens that Anne Mills joins me here one day.

Anne's a year younger than me, maybe seven. A raven-haired Shirley Temple with pale skin, rosy cheeks, and thick eyelashes that curl like a doll's. Her family owns a big brick house in the village with tall porches and high upstairs bedrooms—the kind the Darling children fly from in *Peter Pan*. Though I've never stepped inside, I imagine delicate china teacups, polished silver, and lace curtains. Maids even. The stuff of nobility.

At Brownies, Anne wears the latest fashion: a chocolate brown button-down shirt and culottes, washed and pressed to perfection; a silky white tie knotted precisely so the orange maple leaves float like a breath of autumn across her flat chest. My baggy thrift-store dress is too short in hem and sleeves, poo-hued, and clashes with the immense mustard square that must be ironed and folded in a precise sequence, and then knotted around my neck like a noose and stabbed with a gold, dancing sprite. But now that the Russians have us poised on the brink of nuclear war, a tie that can become a sling or bandage seems like a good idea. It was the English who invented Girlguiding, and they know all about war. Perhaps Anne and I planned this adventure at Brownies. I am the Sixer of the Fairies. Two orange stripes and a succession of merit badges parade down the sleeves of my poo-hued dress.

Anne's family is English. My father wants to be English. But you can't be English just because your stepmother was a war bride, and a string of your Carr ancestors farmed the Yorkshire fen—Celts bred with Vikings—and not English at all except on a map. "English?" my uncle says at my dad's funeral. "Our father was as Irish as Paddy's pig." A carr, I discover, is a marsh overgrown with brush, derived from the Old Norse *kjarr*. It is this carr I claim at the back of our farm. And it is in this carr, my elm lives.

As adventurous as any decent Brownie, Anne climbs Elm that day along with me. Until she gets scared. No amount of cajoling can make her budge. I wonder how she manages to live in her *Peter Pan* bedroom if she's afraid of heights. Finally, I trudge back through the fields to our rural bungalow. There's a car in the driveway. Mrs. Mills stands straight and statuesque, wearing a scowl. Like a good Brownie mother, she marches down the meadow in oxfords and stockings, and after a few harsh words, Anne manages to climb out of Elm's protective arms.

She was never allowed to play with me again—not that Carr kid.

I left Pickering in the early 1970s, before a fungal plague called Dutch Elm Disease wiped out most of the elm trees in Ontario. My parents left not long after, empty nesters seduced by the offer of more money than they'd ever seen in their lives. I don't know if Elm succumbed to the scourge or the developer's saw. Today, the townhouses are stacked for miles on streets named Maple Gate, Cedarcroft, and Linwood—wordy reminders of the past since the trees are gone. Bulldozed. Chipped. Flattened. Vanished like the daisies and the bees. There is no mention of Elm.

That spring—my eighth—*The New Yorker* published excerpts from Rachel Carson's environmental treatise, *Silent Spring.* I didn't hear of it for decades, and when I did, my heart ached for all that once was and will never be again. Yet Carson offers words of encouragement.

"Those who contemplate the beauty of the earth find reserves of strength that will endure as long as life lasts. There is something infinitely healing in the repeated refrains of nature—the assurance that dawn comes after night, and spring after winter."

I believe Carson is right. Though my haven is gone, every blade of grass, daisy petal, and butterfly wing exists in my memory. I will always be the ragtag nymph of the woods. In my vision, I perch in the arms of my dear Elm tree and survey my vanished kingdom, where no muskrats die, no missiles threaten, and our dear Earth continues to spin out her seasons in turquoise and gold.

WRITING TIME & PLACE

Writing Time

Time should not be an impediment to the story but rather work synchronistically. Whether you write past, present, or future is predicated by the characters and plot. Just beware of writing anachronisms when writing history: something that hasn't been invented yet, an idea, or a historical person your characters wouldn't know about.

I prefer the past to the future, so I tend to write historical fiction rather than science fiction. I especially love Neolithic, Iron Age, Medieval, and Viking times. If I could time-travel to the past, I would, even knowing how violent and precarious life was then. That's why I enjoyed going with my characters back to Iron Age Ireland in *To Kill a King*. Be aware that readers notice errors and will let you know if you make a mistake. Of course, if you write the future, no one can tell you that you got it wrong.

One tool I use for all my books is a blank calendar showing the month and year the story takes place. At generalblue.com, you can search several styles of blank grid calendars with dates going as far back as 1800 and as far forward as 2100. You can either download a full-page monthly calendar and pencil in your key points, or you can open a Word document and type right on it. Below is an example. My current work-in-progress begins in September 1924 on the B.C. coast and is anchored on actual historical events during the Rumrunner era. The example is rough, as I've just started writing. Since the characters are traveling by boat, I need to know about the full moon and the tides. You can actually search the moon and tide tables as well.

September 1924

Sunday	Monday	Tuesday	Wednesday	Thursday	Friday	Saturday
	1	2	3	4	5	6
7	8	9	10	11	12	13 Full Moon High tide 4:30pm Low tide 10:00pm Six Mile Roadhouse Meeting with BG
14	15 G buys whiskey Sells 1/3 to M	16 Stormy Night	17 Boat discovered empty/bloody	18	19	20
21	22	23	24	25	26	27
28	29	30				

Writing Place

This summer, I visited the Six Mile Pub in Victoria and the city of Sooke, B.C., which are settings in my rumrunner story. Two things I noticed that couldn't change over time were that the region was very hilly and that, from the southern tip of Vancouver Island, I could see the United States just across the Strait of Juan de Fuca. This is something you can't discover by looking at a map.

I travel to each setting or location I write about. I've crawled into a dolmen, experienced how the Winter Solstice might appear in the passage tomb at Newgrange, laid upon the Hill of Tara, explored Uisneach (Ish-neck), the navel of Ireland, and climbed to the top of Maeve's cairn in Co. Sligo. I've walked across the Alexandra Bridge in Yale, British Columbia, and worked as a lighthouse keeper on the B.C. coast, where I watched hundreds of Pacific white-sided dolphins come down the strait. I've touched the standing stones in Scotland and explored Skara Brae and the Ring of Brodgar in Orkney. And I saw a strange circle of people chanting "Diablo" in the woods at Buntzen Lake. That's how I got the idea to set my Wicca rituals there.

Visiting sacred sites and places of power is one of the pleasures of being an author. I believe that the landscape holds the energy of what has transpired. This implies that locations where a significant battle or massacre took place, like Culloden Field, where British forces killed the Jacobites, retain that memory. In *To Sleep with Stones*, Dylan describes the standing stones with whom he communicates:

Like sacred witnesses, these massive stones take on the essence of the land and the memories of its people. Limited by their inability to move, they see, hear, and absorb, yet cannot act. Trapped by inertia, most are eager to converse, even the fiercest of them. Those who, like men, have seen too much evil and been turned by it. *To Sleep with Stones*

Sacred sites, many of which appear in myths and legends, exist all over the world. There are shrines, temples, and caves; cathedrals and churches; cemeteries, burial grounds, and battlefields; stone circles and standing stones; mountains, waterfalls, islands, and volcanoes; petroglyphs, ruins, and pyramids. If you're fortunate enough to make a pilgrimage to one of these places, please remember to walk with respect and ask permission before taking photographs or touching anything. You can just as easily feel the energy by sitting silently in meditation; in fact, you might learn more that way.

Martin Gray is a photographer and anthropologist who has traveled to power places and sacred sites around the world for most of his life. If you're curious, watch his fascinating interview with the Theosophical Society at sacredsites.com. His website is an incredible resource and worth taking the time to investigate.

But you need not go on a pilgrimage to a sacred site or power place to inform your writing. It happens in the sensory details. For example, while visiting the village where Dylan spent his teenage years, I heard a story about a man who disappeared one day and then returned as a woman. The storyteller was gob-smacked. What it would be like for a gay or transgender boy living in a small village in Scotland? I thought. Then a character appeared, shared their story, and changed everything.

TRY THIS: PLOTTING

"I've written dozens of ground-breaking, genre-bending, revolutionary works of literary brilliance, profound insight and comedic genius. In my head. In the shower. And while driving. Not actually on paper because haha that's not how writing works apparently." Christina Myers

Objectives:

- Get those words on the page

- Write a scene or series of scenes

- Develop your plot

Stop Reading and Start Writing

Writers are readers. That's how we learn about style and craft, rhythm and flow. But sometimes reading can put a kibosh on your own creative process. It's an effective way to procrastinate. Fortunately, sometimes I can't find anything I want to read. In the vast universe of books, nothing stirs me. This is a sign from my inner muse. "It's time to stop reading and start writing," she says.

Sequence

Find a comfortable position in a quiet place with your pen and notebook beside you. Ask spirit what you want to know. Be specific. Close your eyes. *Breathe in. Breathe out.* Time is unimportant. Allow spirit to come in whatever form is needed. Words, movies, conversations, images, and feelings. You'll know when it's time to open your eyes and write, write, write, whatever you experienced. Don't analyze. Don't correct. Just write. Then close your eyes and do it again. And again. You'll know when it's time to get up and stretch.

Then read your words aloud. Then type them. At that point, you can do some flushing and editing.

How I Use This Technique

From my Journal. "I'm writing this in bed by the light of my pink salt lamp. Since midsummer, I've written 72,000 words, almost a novel, in twelve weeks. I found that too much screen time was straining my eyes, so I got new blue lens, and stopped using my computers at night. These two or three hours I used to spend reading novels, I now spend writing my own. I lay in the dark and close my eyes. I ask the question. *What happens now? Show me.* The pictures roll, and when I've watched a while, I open my eyes, grab my pen and scrawl in my notebook. When I've written as much as I can, I lay back down, cover my eyes with an eye pillow, and begin again. Sometimes, I do this several times. I've tossed out three pens in the last week.

Some mornings, as I transcribe onto the computer, I don't remember anything I've written. The jagged scrawl doesn't look like it could come from these fingers. It's like waking from a vivid dream, jotting it all down fast, then reading it a week later. My muse is with me. Whispering and showing me scenes, telling me his story. I stopped blogging, stopped posting on social media, released the pressure, and opened the channels. Now, words flow. Of course, it will need to be filtered, refined, and distilled, but there'll be whiskey from water in the end."

Writing in Sequence

Not everyone writes in sequence. In fact, many writers don't. Diana Gabaldon, of *Outlander* fame is one such example. When you write with your muse, you might receive fragments, phrases, or symbols. You might hear snatches of conversation or a song that suddenly triggers an emotional reaction.

Bits move, get rewritten, and get cut. Sometimes, they return in a wholly different way.

I do write in sequence and use "What happens next?" to cue visuals. I've written my last five books using this technique and have yet to rewrite a plot.

Antidote to Fear: Rejection

NO AGENT OR PUBLISHER WILL EVER ACCEPT MY WRITING. I CAN'T STAND REJECTION.

There are reams of posts online written by writers on the subject of rejection. Some authors keep fat files. In his classic writing memoir, Stephen King says, "By the time I was fourteen (and shaving twice a week whether I needed to or not) the nail in my wall would no longer support the weight of the rejection slips impaled upon it. I replaced the nail with a spike and went on writing."[1]

You can read Fifty Iconic Writers Who Were Repeatedly Rejected[2] or just know that the chances of having your book

---

1. King, Stephen. On Writing — a Memoir of the Craft. Scribner: NY, 2000

2. https://www.onlinecollege.org/2010/05/17/50-iconic-writers-who-were-repeatedly-rejected/

accepted first time by an agent or publisher, no matter how good it is, are similar to catching a cloud in your bare hands.

When I pitched *To Charm a Killer* back around 2010, I had a few bites, but no one swallowed the hook. I was a rookie in those days and just wanted to see my book in print, so after a handful of rejections, I self-published through Lulu.com (a print-on-demand, self-publishing platform). I provided a cover created by my artist friend, Judi Gardnner, and their in-house people did the formatting. It cost a few hundred dollars. Be aware that some presses charge thousands of dollars. Avoid them, and ask an Indie author for advice.

I've learned since then. For example, an agent or publisher will not accept other books in your series if your first book was Independently published unless you've managed to sell several thousand books.

I've also heard horror stories from authors who were traditionally published and now are Indies. Some were dumped. Some wanted more control. Some couldn't get back the copyright to their novels. Some publishers just disappeared.

So, why try?

Though the stigma between traditional and independent publishers is weakening, it still exists.

Traditional publishers often employ excellent house editors and cover designers. They will take a chunk of cash to cover their costs, but Indies pay for everything out of their own pocket.

They usually have a bigger marketing budget and credibility. This means they can organize bigger signings and launches, and get endorsements for your book that could rocket you onto the best sellers list.

They can get you into contests that don't admit Indies that might result in a national award.

If you've been under contract with a traditional publisher, you can apply for grant money to continue writing. This situation is improving as Indie publishing becomes the norm. In Canada, if you belong to the Writers Union of Canada you can apply for funding. WUC uses a six-point system. Last year, I received funding for a public reading, and was approved for a professional development grant from the BC Arts Council. I will continue to apply for funding. If I get rejected, I realize it's because there just isn't enough money to go around.

Try not to take rejection personally. I had one agent say they wouldn't take my book because they didn't have a buyer in that genre at this time. Agents are salespeople. They know their buyers and sometimes gamble on what will sell. The same agent said RomCom was selling last year, but no one knew what would be in demand next year. This is another reason to write for yourself and not for a constantly fluctuating market. Some agents will only look at material from writers they've met personally who've pitched to them at conferences. Other agents only take referrals.

A Note on Indie Publishing

Expect a large learning curve if you decide to Indie publish, but know also, there are a vast array of resources. I've already talked about some of the software (Atticus and Vellum both create beautiful books). This isn't a book about marketing or even formatting your book, so I'll keep this brief. But know that you are capable of publishing your own book. If you're uncomfortable with technology, find someone who is and ask for help. Just beware of what we call "vanity presses"—businesses who say, "Yes, we'd love to publish your book," but then charge you thousands of dollars to do it. Also, beware of contests that charge large entry fees but may not be legit.

One organization worth checking out is Alli, the Alliance of Independent Authors (pronounced ally).[3] Being a member of Alli has many benefits, including discounts, advice, and contract and contest vetting. Alli is generally an Indie author/publisher's best friend. You'll notice I use the term Indie author rather than self-published. That's because there's still a stigma that those of us who Indie publish are working to change.

---

3. https://www.allianceindependentauthors.org/

THE ANTAGONIST

"The more successful the villain, the more successful the picture."
Alfred Hitchcock

To create and sustain tension, your villain or antagonist must be an equal match for your protagonist. Basic story conflict features an engaging protagonist with a goal and a complex antagonist who tries to thwart it. The best stories are ones in which motivations are strong and clear and we understand both characters.

In your high school English class, you may remember hearing about several types of conflict:

Man vs Man
Man vs Self
Man vs Nature
Man vs Society
Man vs Technology
Man vs Supernatural

We're probably most familiar with Man vs Man where the "I want it—you can't have it" motivation drives the conflict. But whether your antagonist is an erupting volcano, an angry whale, a dystopian society, a serial killer, a vengeful vampire, or some dark aspect of the protagonist, they must be an appropriate match, as forceful and driven as your hero. They must also be as complex, so readers need to know them intimately. Even if we don't like the villain, we must understand them.

This means your antagonist needs a strong, clear motive for their actions and a backstory. Serial killers don't just kill. They kill for a reason, and if you can delve into the psychology behind their need to kill, you'll create a more complex story. We need to know not just what is happening but why, and why *now*. Even tornadoes have a backstory.

The villain in three of my Hollystone books is a sixteenth-century vampire. Early on, a beta reader asked, "What makes this vampire different from any other vampires? Why should I care about him?" That question spawned a conversation with Don Diego, during which I learned about his life.

Channel Your Villain

One way to tap into your antagonist's personality and motivation is to create a list of questions and then channel them. Ask them to write you a letter and introduce themselves. When you're channeling them, you'll pick up their voice and tone, as well as any peculiar accents or aspects.

Maybe you can't channel a tornado, but you can ask, "Why is this weather happening in this place and time? What is its genesis? How does it connect with my characters? How does it change their lives?"

Types of Stories

Stories often have more than one conflict. For example, a story with a Man vs. Nature conflict is often a "Superhero" story that also involves a Man vs. Himself conflict. In other words, the hero has to step up and use their skills and talents to save others from whatever natural phenomenon is threatening them.

A wonderful resource for story typing is Blake Snyder's *Save the Cat*[1]. In this thin masterpiece, Snyder explains that there are only ten types of stories produced in Hollywood. He provides the key ingredients and gives examples. It's a fantastic, inspiring read and can help you situate your story in a broader context. For example, I often write quest stories, something Snyder calls the "Golden Fleece."

This type of story originated in Greek mythology with Jason and his Argonauts, who undertake a perilous adventure to find the golden fleece. It features a hero on a time-sensitive journey who assembles a team to help meet a particular goal.

In *To Render a Raven*, when the coven travels by yacht up the Northwest Pacific coast to rescue Estrada's baby from the vampire Diego, they are on a quest. Getting the baby back is the reward, but the trials of the journey are paramount.

I recommend you read *Save the Cat*. It's fascinating and you'll never watch movies the same way again.

---

1. https://savethecat.com/

Consider the movie *Jaws*. Yes, the shark is evil and eating anyone who goes into the water, but the mayor is the real antagonist, as he refuses to listen to Sheriff Brody and close the beaches while they sort out the problem. It becomes a Golden Fleece quest when Brody organizes a team (Hooper and Quint) to confront and kill the shark. The conflict is Man vs Nature but also Man vs Man, and Man vs Himself as Brody must face his greatest fears and confront the shark alone in the end.

WRITING SEX SCENES WITH YOUR MUSE

"Graze on my lips, and if those hills be dry, Stray lower, where pleasant fountains lie." Shakespeare, *Venus and Adonis*

Shakespeare wrote plays designed to entertain masses of people of all classes who were only too familiar with love, sex, and death. His sexual puns and innuendoes are famous and can still make us crack a smile. The Bard knew his audience and what was required of his genre, and we writers can learn much from the master.

Although it's not required, the expectations of the genre frequently determine whether or not you should include sex in your book. For example, readers of romance, historical fiction, and urban fantasy all expect some type of sexual encounters ranging from sweet to explicit. So, how do you, as an author, write a sex scene with your muse?

I thought my writing was explicit until I read a few romances written by friends that *were* explicit. Now, I call my stories steamy, meaning if you were reading in your car, you might breathe a little deeper and steam up your windows. When I wrote the first draft of *Lure*, there were no sex scenes at all. Since I was writing romantic suspense, my editor advised me to include at least one near the end as there was a buildup throughout. It would be anticlimactic not to have it.

I follow my own rules when it comes to writing about sex but here are a few considerations:

DECIDE WHAT HEAT LEVEL YOU'RE PREPARED TO WRITE. In "sweet" stories, sex happens off the page. There are also "spicy" stories, "steamy" stories, and some that are "explicit." I take cues from my characters. Whatever you decide to write, own it.

USE A DESCRIPTIVE SETTING. Sexy scenes can happen pretty much anywhere and rarely occur in the protagonist's bed. Unless it's the next morning. I don't plan the setting. That's up to my muse. Pretend you're a video camera and zoom in and out.

DON'T BE GRATUITOUS. Sex scenes appear for a reason. Mine are always part of an action-reaction sequence that drives the plot, and there are often consequences.

DON'T BE TOO PHYSICALLY DETAILED (unless you're writing about explicit sex). Sensory cues show us what's taking place. Make it artistic. I rarely name body parts during a love scene. We glean much from body language and can follow the movement of hands and lips across necks, thighs, and bellies without explaining where they're landing and what they're doing. For example, when someone drops to their knees, we usually know what's coming. Avoid close-ups of the pleasant fountains.

Lovemaking is the height of emotion. We want to know what the characters are thinking and feeling through expressive dialogue, bodily sensations, and inner thoughts.

Foreplay is more intriguing than the main event. The longer the tease, the more intense the actual joining will be.

Make sex consensual. I don't write rape scenes. In *To Charm a Killer*, Maggie is *almost* raped. Innocent and naive, she gets herself into a situation and then can't get out. Anyone who's experienced date rape can relate. It's a coming-of-age story, and in this moment, she learns much about herself and the world. I drew on personal experiences from my teen years to write that scene. Maggie's fortunate enough to get rescued. Most of us aren't.

Write from your character's point of view. This means you're inside their head, seeing through their eyes, and thinking and feeling their experience. Close your eyes, merge with them, and go with it. If you feel the raw emotion, your reader will too. Enough said.

Add internal conflict. Often, people who fall in love feel conflicted. If you can express this personal conflict, it raises the stakes. Do they feel guilty? Afraid? Anxious? Ask your character what's really going on in this moment. Then run with it.

Shed your moral cap and stop worrying about your mother. I'm a mother and grandmother, and most mothers I know love my sex scenes. Write, smile, and enjoy.

PART 4

THE ECHOING MUSE

Writing to Heal

"While I've never lived in a pre-industrialized dystopian empire like Elarhe in Lover, Destroyer, he and I both know what it's like to be an outcast, to mourn a murdered friend, to be homeless, and to yearn for things that seem beyond your grasp. While I've never destroyed an entire kingdom like Kite, his shame and insecurity resonate with me because it's how I felt when the relative who sexually abused me died when I was sixteen. I didn't feel as relieved as I did ashamed—like I had somehow killed him with my quiet, clumsy rage." Sionnach Wintergreen

Something writers do naturally and repeatedly is write through their trauma. Writing allows us to speak our truth through the voice of another. In writing, we don a mask and slay our demons. We delve into the emotions we'd prefer to keep buried. But delve we must, because acknowledging trauma sparks healing. That's why the #MeToo campaign stirred so many people. To stand up and say those two words diminished the power of the secret and brought the act to its knees. #MeToo.

Whether we write poetry or memoir, fiction or song lyrics, writing helps us heal. In these truthful moments when we bare our soul to the world, the reader acts as a witness and in healing our own trauma, we also help others heal. Writing makes it safe. You can write out your demons without exposing yourself to further demonization. You can wear the trickster mask and drop bombs in snitches and snatches.

Write Through Your Trauma

In *To Render a Raven*, Estrada experiences the loss of his child when a vampire kidnaps her. Don't worry. After a long journey up the Pacific coast by yacht and a tremendous ordeal, he and Sensara get her back unscathed. The vampires in this story symbolize all the evil in this world which I cannot put into words. Who else would steal a child from her bed on the eve of her first birthday? Only something otherworldly from the darkest and grimmest of faerie tales.

On one level, I'm writing urban fantasy. But on another level, I'm writing to heal from my own experience of loss. I, too, lost a child. I know the pain of separation. I remember the grief I felt when I left my ex-husband and my son decided to stay with his dad. I remember the moment I experienced the severing of our mother-son bond. Some moments never leave you. Time stops, and scars spring up like a wall of thorns. We remain estranged in the physical world, though we must be connected by a mother-son bond. We have to be.

Have you lost someone? Left someone behind? Their face, like a photograph, becomes indelibly etched in memory and never changes. This is the lair of my Inner Muse, who conjures up what she needs in order to heal.

Red Pajamas
You come to me in red pajamas,
Blond bangs curling, catching lashes.
Eyes like mine as blue as moonstone,
Dripping salt like captured sea foam.
Caught between the now and then
You were just ten. My boy of ten.
Alone. Afraid. Abandoned. Aching.
In my dreams you're shaking, breaking.
Wicked world so wedged between us—
Dead we dwelt in separate regions.
Built up walls to ward off sadness
Dripping rocks that held our madness.
Grief stalks still in red pajamas
Tortured tears catch in my lashes.
Twelve years lost. I haven't known you—
Still I love you. Ache to hold you.
Then you come in red pajamas
Always ten in red pajamas.

ANTIDOTE TO FEAR: CRITICISM

Yes, people will judge you. Both positively and negatively. You might get some bad reviews. You might get your buttons pushed. I now know exactly what my buttons are. And, no doubt, people will look at you differently. Because you're an author.

Remember what courage it takes to write. Yes, you're exposing yourself. But you're also touching lives with your work and making people think, feel, and, perhaps, heal.

My Hollystone Mysteries are urban fantasy mysteries and thrillers for teens and adults. They're sexy books that push boundaries. Whose job is it to push boundaries, if not the artist? My hero is a bisexual, polyamorous magician. I tell his stories, go where he goes, follow his quests, and experience his experiences. The series revolves around his personal relationships as he tries to save the people he loves, and he often expresses his feelings sexually. So, yes, people sometimes hear that I write LGBTQ+ books and judge me without getting to know me or reading my books.

Sometimes, you might get a bad review. I have a friend who refers to these people as trolls. They pop out and attack you, then disappear back under their bridges. It usually occurs on social media, where, unfortunately, it stays. The only remedy is to ignore it and remember the positive things people say. Unless you're a Hobbit, you can't fight a troll. As a reader, I love some books. I've also thrown books across the room. But I'll decline to review rather than write a bad review because I know what it takes to write a book. One of the most positive things I did was copy my best reviews to my website. Seeing them all listed made me feel wonderful.

I've also heard of writers being gang-attacked on social media (especially Twitter). I imagine it's as humiliating as a public flogging or being bombarded with rotten fruit while you stand bent with your head and hands in the stocks. You may need to grow skin like a pineapple rather than a peach. But don't let this fear stop you from writing what you're inspired to write.

When I read *Outlander*, Diana Gabaldon became one of my heroes because she wrote the story she needed to tell. Being a writer takes courage. Let the rewards outweigh the fear.

Music as Muse

"I don't know how I got to write those songs . . . Those early songs were almost magically written. It's a different kind of penetrating magic." Bob Dylan[1]

Writing music can feel like magic, like a gift from the gods. Inviting music to be your muse can have a similar effect.

Music as Muse

My earliest musical inspiration occurred during Sunday services, when my feet dangled from a wooden pew at St. Paul's Anglican Church. I soaked up those lyrical hymns and the poetry of the St. James Bible, sang in the choir, and started plunking out tunes on the church organ.

"The child is father of the man," Wordsworth wrote in 1802, meaning that what we experience in childhood shapes who we become.

---

1. FULL 60 Minutes, Ed Bradley 2004 Interview

Neuroscientists at USC[2] now say that listening to music as a child and learning to play a musical instrument accelerate brain development around language. Sound vibrations received by the ear send signals to the brain and stimulate auditory pathways. The ability of a child to determine tone, rhythm, and pitch is enhanced.

I'm convinced that my early exposure to music and literature has positively affected my life. I started piano lessons at around nine after my father noticed my progress on the church organ, and by fourteen, I'd completed eight grades of piano. Years later, when I lived with my musical husband, I learned to play chord progressions and started writing songs.

Music is one of my strongest muses.

Sound as Muse

Writing is not just a scattering of words on a page. Those words travel through the eyes and brain of the reader and emerge as sound bytes. Music.

There is a syllabic rhythm, a beat to the sounds. When you read aloud, you can *hear* if the words work in harmony, if the sentence should be inverted, cut, lengthened, or if the pause is held by an ellipsis, cut by a period, or merged with a comma.

---

2. https://news.usc.edu/102681/childrens-brains-develo
   p-faster-with-music-training/

Poets and songwriters have always played with rhythms, beats, and syllables. In the earliest days, drum beats, plucked strings, and crotal bells accompanied the bard. Later, poets began counting beats per line and writing in intricate patterns. Ballad. Sonnet. Villanelle.

Fiction is as musical as songwriting or poetry. Sounds intertwine and press against each other like lovers.

A similar beat defines the plot, stressing emotions, so the reader feels the musicality of the character's feelings and thoughts as they navigate the rise and fall of action. Diminished reflections follow major skirmishes. Life is ups and downs, peaks and valleys, like a melody. People move in harmony or discord, sometimes reaching crescendos.

The more you listen to good music, no matter the genre, your spirit will soak up this knowingness. It will strengthen your clairaudient gifts, and you'll become clairsentient to the musicality of writing—meaning, you'll just know it.

You don't have to grow up playing an instrument to feel its benefits, but if you can expose yourself and/or your child to music, there are multiple benefits. The healing benefits are extraordinary, as any music therapist will tell you. My father said, he always knew what mood I was in when he came home from work because of what I was playing on the piano and how I approached it.

Using Sound to Write

Beyond listening, here are a few other ways to involve sound in your writing process:

COMPILE A PLAYLIST for your work in progress that triggers the desired tone or mood. You can do this through a streaming program like Spotify. While writing *To Dance with Destiny*, I created a bluesy playlist called "Estrada's Flat on the Drive," which you can access through Spotify.[3]

RECORD AUDIO FILES—conversations, music, ideas, phrases, lines, or nature sounds. Much of my inspiration happens when I'm out walking in the woods or by water. I've heard other writers, particularly poets, say the same thing. Away from modernity and surrounded by nature, we slow our thoughts as in meditation and move into Theta-brain where we can hear the voice of the muse. The challenge is to get those precious words on paper. Most of us carry the answer in our pocket. Turn on your phone and record audio files. If you don't have a phone, pack a journal and pencil. Sit and capture these moments. I've recorded a lullaby, plot-related epiphanies, and many character conversations in this way. My characters/muses are very chatty on walks. I'm never alone.

If you think people will think you're weird, embrace it. Writers *are* weird. *Wyrd* in the Old English sense of the word which relates to fate or destiny, your own and that of your subjects. The Weird Sisters in *Macbeth* were said to control destiny. Let your inner witch run free. But if you're still worried about being judged, observe all the people talking on their phones while they walk. You're engaging in a conversation just like that woman over there.

---

3. https://open.spotify.com/playlist/1eEwe6g7woMZ1JH ciRf7sZ

USE MUSICAL WRITING TOOLS. One of the writing practices I describe in this book is a shamanic journey. When I first started working with the shamanic journey technique, I bought an MP3 called *Traditional Shamanic Drum Journey* by Tim Norton. The solo drumming in the sound clips is a trigger that facilitates spiritual travel. I particularly like Norton's work because he offers three journeys and incorporates rattles and other mystical sounds into a consistent drumbeat. It's also available on YouTube and Spotify, so you can try it. I think this is a "love it or hate it" experience. I recommend small doses in a specific setting when you're ready to work. I've shared my journeys in two sections: "Symbols and Archetypes" and "Allies and Animals."

CREATE CHARACTERS WHO ARE MUSICIANS OR LOVE MUSIC. This forces you to do research. Make your protagonist a guitarist or a jazz aficionado like Harry Bosch. In *To Charm a Killer*, Maggie goes to Ireland to search for her grandfather, who is a trad musician. To research this book, I traveled to Ireland and I learned to play traditional Irish music on my guitar. Our little group of musicians toured in Co. Clare, where I sang ballads in pubs. First-hand experience is the best research. Feel it, don't just read about it.

FIND YOUR MUSICAL AND LYRICAL MUSES. You know who they are. What are they here to tell you? In *To Kill a King*, Conall Ceol is a Celtic bard from Iron Age Ireland. His character is inspired by one of my bardic muses, Peter Gabriel. Though I can't travel to Iron Age Ireland— I sure wish I could—Simon and Maria O'Dwyer[4] offer listening opportunities on their website. And, of course, every time I listen to Peter Gabriel sing "Mercy Street," "In your Eyes," or "Here Comes the Flood," I'm transported to scenes featuring Conall. Peter Gabriel is my spiritual elixir and a potent force in my life.

WRITE ABOUT THAT WHICH CAPTURES YOUR HEART. The bards of old wrote history as it happened. You can explain and inform in a way that evokes emotion and delivers a message without being didactic. What captures your heart?

---

4. https://www.ancientmusicireland.com/

Literature as Muse

"I don't know which is more discouraging, literature or chickens." E.B. White, *Charlotte's Web*

I taught high school English for many years, and I know White's statement to be true. At some point in your life, in one of your English classes, you've been forced to respond creatively to a piece of literature. English teachers love that kind of assignment. Think of it not as a writing task but as writing fan fiction. Here are a few ways to use literature as your muse.

Read Widely

When you read, your vocabulary will deepen. You discover new words, and sometimes they even stick. If you use an E-reader, you can track new vocabulary on your tablet. For years, I've jotted down "words that dazzle" in the back of my journal.

Play with Style

Experiment with writing in the voice of a poet or author who inspires you.

We all write with our own unique voice, but find a writer who inspirers you and experiment with writing in their voice or style. It's like trying on a costume. And, when you find a particular poet or author you love, read everything you can by them—not to copy or become them but to digest the corn husk they offer. And always, always quote and credit the writer.

Write Fan Fiction

Millionaire EL James originally wrote *Fifty Shades of Gray* as *Twilight* fan fiction, and Cassandra Clare first became famous writing *Harry Potter* fan fiction. Enough said. If you've never heard of these writers, don't worry about it. If you want to try your hand at writing fan fiction, choose a world of characters you know well and spin off it into an original piece. It doesn't have to be something from popular culture; just choose something you're passionate about.

Springboard from the Classics

This happens frequently with Jane Austen. I hope it makes her smile to know that centuries later, fans are writing spin-offs and sequels to her work. I just discovered "Dracula Beyond Stoker" (DBS Publishing), which is looking for Dracula-inspired works. If you love the classics, you can bet that someone else does too. Write what you're drawn to, and let literature be your muse.

In my medieval literature class, I wrote a response to *Beowulf* in the voice of the woman he left behind when he went to find glory by killing the monster Grendel. I suppose it's ancient fan fiction.

Play with Form

When I was teaching English literature, I wrote poetry in many forms. Why? Because when you read it, you naturally start to write it.

This is a modified Italian Sonnet I wrote in response to Dan Brown's *DaVinci Code*. It has a particular structure and rhyme scheme, but within it is a tribute to the Mary Magdalene Dan Brown conjured.

The Plight of the Magdalene
Through blackened veils of time, I search for shards
Of hidden truth, through tales of terror wild,
Of cross-torn love and Magdalene defiled.
Fierce persecution by his Roman guards
Portentous torture foretold by the stars.
A desperate widow flees engorged with child
To Egypt, while Old Caesar stands beguiled.
Sequestered symbols hide in gypsy cards.
But Brother Joseph shields the blessed pair.
For twelve long years they tread the Pharaoh's sands
And then in southern France the vessel lands
Where Hebrew Princess Sarah blossoms fair
Uniting with her Merovingian King

As Christ her Father and his Angels sing.
So sacrilegious scholars weave the tale
Of weeping Magdalene, most Holy Grail.

Playing with different forms and genres can invite new muses into your life. Many people writing Creative Non-Fiction or Memoir are experimenting with form.

I attended an impressive presentation by Nicole Breit[1] while studying Creative Non-Fiction. If you're exploring memoir, explore Breit's courses. She teaches ten different essay forms and posits that working within a form is inspirational in itself.

---

1. https://www.nicolebreit.com/

MEMORY AS MUSE

"When it was suggested that I write a memoir I said, 'I'm not old enough. I'm not distinguished enough.' But I went home and sat down to write, and the material for the book just came flooding into my hands." Julia Cameron

What is Memoir?

A memoir is a series of interconnected vignettes or episodes that wind around one central theme from an individual's life. *Yours.* It often whispers a profound message to the world that is positive, uplifting, and inspiring. You may have experienced a hard life where there were dark moments, and you can absolutely write about them, but from those trials, readers want to see learning and healing.

A memoir is a simple Hero's Journey. There are allies and enemies, tests and trials—perhaps an ordeal from which you didn't think you'd surface. But in the end, the hero (you) must survive and arrive home (whatever that means to you) with the elixir of truth (the message).

Tips and Tricks for Writing Memoirs

THINK OF A SIMPLE OVERARCHING THEME ABOUT LIFE that you can illustrate with interwoven episodes from your personal memories. Choose two or three themes and meditate on them.

Here are some possibilities from my life that wend their way through my memories in one way or another:

•Life is eternal. Angels and spirits walk among us, influence us, and connect when we need them most.

•Nature is a powerful force who offers comfort, healing, and inspiration, unless . . .

•Animals can open our hearts through unconditional love.

•Family relationships are a complex roadmap to distant epiphanies.

•Magic happens when we believe and even when we do not.

MEDITATE. ENGAGE IN MIND-MAPPING WITH YOUR MUSE. What memories present themselves? They will likely be the ones that carry the most meaning and emotion.

REVEAL YOUR TRUTH. People often advise memoir writers to be honest, but honestly, truth is a matter of perspective. This is a story from your eyes, so describe what *you* remember. If you could time-travel back to the moment and hover from above, what happened might be completely different from the memory you hold. Moreover, other people will likely see something particular about themselves and their relationship to the incidents. My sister and I, who are six years apart, hold very different memories of our family life. Remember, this is your memory and your memoir. So, describe it as you remember it, with all the feelings and emotions it triggers.

REVEAL YOUR PERSONALITY, FEARS, CORE BELIEFS, STRENGTHS, AND FLAWS. As in all stories, a natural change should occur and arc from beginning to middle to end within each piece and in the entire compilation. You are the protagonist, but other characters should also be realistic and complex. Avoid using real names and making characters recognizable unless you obtain permission. This can be a legal or ethical issue, so if in doubt, consult a lawyer.

WRITE CONVERSATIONALLY AND DON'T CENSOR YOURSELF. Swear when necessary. Use the language of the time. For example, when I wrote as a teenager in the early Seventies, I wrote about plastic people (urban adults with tiny boxed-in minds who live in square boxes and use Tupperware). Apparently, my hippie soul was onto something since plastic is the cause of one of our current catastrophes.

START IN MEDIA RES—IN THE MIDST OF THE ACTION. Take us right to an image and a moment.

USE FLASHBACKS SPARINGLY, offering only enough information so the reader can understand.

USE SENSORY LANGUAGE TO TAKE US WITH YOU ON YOUR JOURNEY. Incorporate all the senses: sight, taste, sound, smell, touch, and yes, even that sixth sense, the clairs.

ADD HUMOR. Even a smile releases endorphins that lower our stress levels. That's a beautiful gift to yourself and your reader.

Here's an example of a published memoir piece I wrote a few years ago. It fits the theme, "family relationships are a complex roadmap to epiphanies."

Smoky Moments

My father used to leave his large packs of cigarettes lying open on the counter beside the electric stove. Its plain gray surface was pocked by the still smoldering ends of forgotten butts that had slipped from their precarious lodgings in the tan-stained ashtray, careened off the side, and burned black holes in the arborite. It was a bane to my mother. "Oh Bill," she would cry. I wondered if it was the mess of her sacred cooking counter or simply the mess of my father that frustrated her so much.

The cigarettes themselves were simple to pocket yet hard to smoke. Still, they beckoned me. Sometimes, they were Player's Plain in the brilliant turquoise box; other times, they were Export Plain in the forest green box emblazoned with the Highland lassie in her Scottish garb. Surely, they were instruments of myth: keys to some ancient and forgotten time where tribal lords battled for power and women. Commonly known as truck driver cigarettes—my father had long outgrown filter tips—they were the most sinister and seductive cigarettes conceivable to a fourteen-year-old girl.

I remember my father crouched in the dusky doorway of the barn after supper, smoking and drifting like a wizard. He could never abide female chatter; particularly, my mother's. A lay minister, he had verses to interpret and sermons to write, or perhaps he just preferred the company of cattle.

Sometimes, I would come singing around the corner of my playhouse and stop dead, ashamed to discover him sitting smoking in the old, cobwebbed outhouse, pants at his knees, chin resting on a fist. Like a backwoods Buddha, he never flinched, while I slunk off, pretending I had not caught my father in the crapper once again.

I began by pocketing a smoke or two at a time, along with a box of sulfurous wooden matches, and smoked them leisurely out on the trail where I went horseback riding. My old buckskin never minded, and they took me places I'd never ventured alone. I still love the scent of a cigarette in the open air of springtime, although I can't abide it any other way. It cuts through stale layers of memory, evoking images of budding leaves, burgundy trilliums, cawing crows, and churning creek beds, and reminds me that, even then, I was obsessed with knowing who I was and why I was here. The purpose-driven delinquent. Drifting on smoky wings, I was the witch of Stoney Creek.

My father never said anything about the stolen cigarettes, though he must have known. Then again, he never really said much to me at all. After a while, I took to buying my own cigarettes with my babysitting money. A pack of Rothman's King Size cost fifty cents at Stella's store. I had been frequenting Stella's since I was old enough to buy a five-cent banana popsicle with my berry-picking cash. Her prices were high as she was an independent grocer, so my parents never shopped there. Whether she would have turned me in or not, I neither questioned nor cared.

By fifteen, I was smoking in my bedroom closet with the window cracked. Eventually, my mother discovered my ashtray full of butts, and the anguished cry of "Oh Bill" resounded. My father promptly announced that while I lived in his house, I would follow his rules. When I was sixteen and legal, I could do whatever I wanted, but until then, I was to do as I was told. Fortunately, my sixteenth birthday arrived not long after, and I celebrated by settling into my father's armchair and lighting a cigarette.

My father spent his final months in a hospital that stunk of urine, near blind, capturing butterflies in a world of his own creation. After his passing at Easter 1996, the doctors informed us he had lung cancer. I quit smoking that year for the second time in my life.

Yet still, I wander beneath a leafy veil of who and why and how, and long for bygone days of forest trails and smoky moments, when a kid could steal a cigarette and think she got away with something.

Travel as Muse

My Family and Other Animals by Gerald Durrell is the first travel book I fell in love with. In this family chronicle, young Gerry explores the flora and fauna on the Greek island of Corfu when his eccentric English family sells their home in Britain and moves to paradise. Written as a series of anecdotes, Durrell draws the reader in with his storytelling skills, eccentric characters, attention to detail, humor, wit, and forays into zoology. A hilarious and poignant memoir-travel writing book, you can also find it as the first book in *The Corfu Trilogy*—757 pages that will warm your heart through the most frigid winter. This book is largely responsible for Greece being scrawled on my bucket list.

Great travel writing triggers our bohemian souls and allows us to tag along from beneath the comfort of a quilt or the security of an armchair. In some cases, travel writing can inspire you to climb out of that chair and travel yourself.

I'm not a travel writer per se, but I've traveled and written. Most of my adventures land in my books in one way or another. Sometimes my travel inspires a story; other times I travel to a particular place because of the story I'm writing.

Here are a few suggestions to deepen your travel writing experience:

When you read books by notable travel writers, read like a writer and not just a reader. Ask yourself: What are they doing, and how are they doing it?

I recently attended a webinar that featured Bill Arnott[1] and Mark Abley,[2] two bestselling authors who've made their mark in travel writing. Both men found success writing about places off the beaten path. Though they employ enough journalistic skill to place us in the setting, their writing is fresh and unique, often lyrical and literary, empathetic, humorous, historical, and experimental. They craft entire books, and in Arnott's case, Viking sagas, that move beyond the travel article into enthralling storytelling.

If you're interested in becoming a travel writer, Lindy Alexander offers behind-the-scenes interviews with travel writers in this post on The Freelancer's Year.[3]

Avoid traveling as a tourist. This is easier said than done, I know, but engaging with the locals and living as they do inspires a richer perspective. That means veering off the tourist trail. There are several ways to accomplish this; some of which are economically advantageous. I recently

---

1. https://billarnottaps.wordpress.com/

2. http://markabley.com/

3. https://thefreelancersyear.com/blog/travel-journalis m-life-of-travel-writer/

heard of a couple who travel the world as Trusted House and/or Pet Sitters.[4] Sitters pay an annual membership fee, and are vetted and reviewed.

When my daughter and I first traveled to Ireland in 2005, we joined Willing Workers on Organic Farms.[5] She wanted to live in Ireland for a while and we thought this might be one way to do it. We visited Eagles Flying[6] in County Sligo, where she was offered a position, but she'd fallen in love with Galway. Once she obtained work in a Galway cafe, she secured a Working Holiday Visa (open to Canadian 18-35 years of age) and stayed for a year.

KEEP A TRAVEL DIARY. Don't just include where you went; jot down your feelings and experiences, odd conversations, things that struck you about the place, humorous moments, and disastrous moments. Travel is not all sugary romance. Be honest, and capture it all. You may not have time to write articles while traveling, but you'll want those detailed notes to invoke your memories when you do sit down to write.

RESEARCH THE HISTORY AND GEOGRAPHY. Go beyond what's in the brochure at the hotel, B&B, museum or gallery, and be open to stories. You never know when or where a muse will arise.

CREATE A TRAVEL BLOG TO PUBLISH YOUR PHOTOGRAPHS AND ANECDOTES. Many travel writers post articles online. I

---

4. https://www.trustedhousesitters.com/

5. https://wwoof.net/

6. https://www.eaglesflying.com/

worked as a relief lighthouse keeper at several stations around Vancouver Island in 2013–2014. Before venturing out, I created a blog called Life on the BC Lights[7] to record my adventures. Since then, I've used those experiences to write a novel.

MOVE QUIETLY THROUGH AN UNKNOWN CULTURE WITH CURIOSITY AND EMPATHY. Cast off your cloak of entitlement and get out of your comfort zone as you explore the reality of a place and its people. Don't be that tourist grimacing at the local food while demanding fish and chips.

LEARN AS MUCH LANGUAGE AS POSSIBLE. Enroll in language classes before and during your stay, practice, and don't be shy. Try out your humble skills in the local markets. People appreciate your willingness to try.

APPLY FOR A WRITING RESIDENCY. Explore the Writers' Trust of Canada[8] for opportunities in Canada. Some are residencies in private homes, others in public libraries, and still others in universities. Res Artis[9] offers international writing residencies worth pursuing, especially if you're curious to research a particular country. Most residencies require that you're willing and able to teach or mentor other writers while you're there.

---

7. http://lifeonthebclights.blogspot.com/

8. https://www.writerstrust.com/programs/residency-p rograms/

9. https://resartis.org/

TAKE TIME TO MEDITATE. This will decrease stress, help you remain balanced, and signal to your muses that you're open to inspiration.

USE SENSORY LANGUAGE. As I described in "Sensory Word Weaving," you want to evoke the atmosphere of the place by showing the reader how it feels. Experiment with new descriptors and metaphors to avoid clichés.

WRITE CONVERSATIONALLY IN FIRST PERSON. This is your personal travel experience, so tell the story from your point of view. Interject dialogue and make it your own.

OFFER TIPS AND ADVICE. One of the purposes of travel writing is to inspire others to visit the places you've been. Make your story relatable and offer navigational tips, bits of historical background, and cultural insights.

REVISE AND EDIT. Whether you want to Indie-publish on your own blog or find a home elsewhere for your travel writing, revising and editing are crucial.

PITCH YOUR ARTICLES AND IDEAS. If your endgame is to publish, you need to pitch. Some travel writers actually get paid, while others get free flights, accommodations, or entry fees covered in exchange for an article. If that's your goal, I suggest you join a serious travel writing group and do some research. In this case, you'd pitch before you travel. Other times, you might write the article and pitch it when you return. Mad for W.B. Yeats on my second trip to Ireland in 2006, I wrote "Conjuring Yeats." Literary Traveler[10] liked

---

10. https://www.literarytraveler.com/articles/yeats_irela nd/

my approach and published it. My experiences fleshed out *To Charm a Killer*, the first book in my Hollystone Mysteries series.

EXPERIMENT WITH FORMS. Travel writing falls into the creative nonfiction genre, and appears in many forms. As I mentioned in "Literature as Muse," playing with different forms and genres can invite new muses into your life. You might explore different forms of the essay, write a letter, infuse your work with poetry or sketches, or merge forms into something entirely your own that speaks to the moment.

While wandering in the footsteps of Yeats, we visited Coole Park[11] in the town of Gort, County Galway. Former owner, Lady Augusta Gregory, was a playwright and folklorist who co-founded the Abby Theatre in 1899. Her estate was a meeting place for writers involved in the Irish Literary Revival. W.B. Yeats, Edward Martyn, George Bernard Shaw, John Millington Synge, and Seán O'Casey all signed the autograph tree in the walled courtyard. Yeats wrote five poems set in the beautiful woods. Coole Park is a sacred place, and while meditating there, I wrote this lyrical letter in which I addressed the Lady herself.

---

11. https://www.coolepark.ie/history/lady-gregory-of-co ole/

It's August at Coole

Black cows break from ivy-braided trees, crisscross our
path, and peer from leafy bowers in the Seven Woods.
While in the stonewalled pasture, a big-racked buck
grazes lazily amongst his harem.
Wild cows and docile deer.
Nature topsy-turvy.
Like Ireland.

There are no wild swans. Not nine and fifty. Not two.
Not even one.
Horseflies harangue us, freed from swaying heads of
purple loosestrife.
Where is this still brimming water?
The tide is out. Sunlight shimmers, waves, and ripples
through my lens and distant trees appear as shaggy
skulking arrows.

We are alone here on the strand. Tara writing poetry on
her Burren rock, and I, courting the ghost of Yeats.

Augusta Gregory has passed away, Bohemian crown
askew. Royal Lady, heiress to the unimagined, patroness
of poets, poet herself and playwright, dearest friend
and grandmum. Molding all in ink-stained hands.
But no Victoria.

Desperate Creatrix. The center did not hold.
Your home was demolished in the widening gyre.
All that remains are Yeats' immortal words etched on
plastic posts. His vision revealed. Arrows point the
tourists here and there through your memories.

Your autograph tree now numbered and analyzed, imprisoned behind iron bars, tagged and martyred like Patrick Pearse.

Do you mind, Great Lady? People still come, to know, to feel, to walk in the footsteps of your poets and playwrights: Synge, Æ, Shaw, Auden … Yeats.

Children play football and hang like fools, dogs chase sticks, dirty your walkways, and life spirals on.

Lough Cuil is Irish now. Comforted by stone and sea, sun, rain, and western winds. Stories resurrected in the Gaeltacht. And your small patch of Ireland breathes still, a sanctuary of green. No withered boughs.

I miss him too, but feel him somehow in the worded wind, and my throat aches.

Yeats.

This is August at Coole.

Antidote to Fear: Success

An Introvert's Nightmare

IF I'M SUCCESSFUL, I'LL HAVE TO CLIMB OUT OF MY CAVE AND SELL MYSELF. I'M WAY TOO INTROVERTED AND SHY TO SPEAK IN PUBLIC.

I've saved this for last as it's my greatest challenge. And so I ask you: Are you hobbling your writing career? Are you afraid that becoming a successful writer will mean you have to change out of your comfy pjs, stand up in front of people, be witty and charming, and talk about your work? Go to conferences? Teach workshops on different aspects of writing? Hobnob in rooms full of other writers, publishers, editors, and performers? Do you consciously or subconsciously resist success? I say subconsciously because a thought is a form of energy as strong as the spoken word.

You may be saying "I'm a writer. I wrote this book." You can hold it up. You can even smile because you're proud of your accomplishment. But your vibration—which is what the listener or viewer feels—is screaming, "I wrote this book but I'm afraid to move forward! What will it mean if I suddenly get famous?"

Take a deep breath.

First of all, fame is rare. You don't have to venture out and market your book. You can continue to live your life, write because it's your passion, and share your work with family and friends.

In reality, most authors don't earn enough money from writing to make a living, even if they're actively marketing. I know authors who are counselors, police officers, teachers, doctors, animal workers, midwives, and lighthouse keepers. Others have a supportive partner with a good job or are retired. Some writers are entrepreneurs who use their books to sell online classes or videos, though I suspect some of them are extraverts. I know other authors whose work in the writing business adds to their success. They are coaches, editors, proofreaders, ghostwriters, writers-in-residence, and copywriters. Other authors host retreats and/or present workshops. Success is personal and writer-specific. You can feel successful without pushing the limits of your comfort zone, so don't let the fear of going public, stop you from writing your book.

As a highly sensitive Introvert, I've learned through negative experiences and spent considerable time exploring ways to reduce anxiety while marketing my books. Here are a few suggestions:

KNOW THYSELF. I enjoy attending conferences, but they're exhausting. Know your limits and plan accordingly. Listen to your body and soul.

TAKE CONTROL OF FOMO (FEAR OF MISSING OUT). Connections are sometimes made at the bar during conferences, but that much stimulation can destroy an Introvert. Decide what you can handle and what you can't. Take time to be alone. Go for a walk in the park. Go out to eat by yourself or with one friend. If you're staying in a hotel, go up to your room and rest. Skip the evening parties or pop in for one drink and schmooze strategically.

START SMALL. If you'd like to present a workshop, start small. Try your local library. If you want to be part of a conference, sign up for a panel. That way, you don't have to hold the entire floor in your hands. As part of a group discussion, you can sit back and listen, then speak when you feel comfortable.

SELL AT LOCAL MARKETS. It's always good to sell books in your own community. When you're behind your table, there's a feeling of security, and you can talk one-on-one with potential buyers. Local craft markets are good for sales. People enjoy chatting with the author about their books and writing experiences. One of the reasons I wrote this book is because I've met so many would-be writers at markets, who don't know how to begin. Someone once told me that two minutes spent talking with a potential buyer surpasses sales through social media. That's been my experience.

CONNECT WITH BOOKSTORES. Introduce yourself to the owner or manager of the local independent bookstore. Some bookstores pay outright for books; while others work on consignment. Either way, it's passive income, and you can be home writing in your pajamas while someone buys your book. If it feels right, inquire about doing a reading or a signing. Many independent bookstores are happy to help you launch your book and have established customers. It means business for them and you.

Conquer your Fear of Public Speaking. I know this is easier said than done. When I first started teaching high school English, I thought I was literally having a heart attack. Eventually, it got easier, although I was still drained at the end of the day. Teaching four classes a day in a school with twelve hundred teens is truly an Introvert's nightmare. But there are supportive programs like Toastmasters that will help you overcome your fear of public speaking. Always practice and rehearse what you're going to say.

Learn to Enjoy Reading Aloud. Public readings are a great way to promote your book. Often, there's a small audience and a host to introduce you, so you need only take a deep breath and begin. The applause at the end is worth it. You may even qualify for a grant.

Be Selective with Social Media. Do your research and apply to podcasts that are a good fit and feel friendly. You may experience the same amount of anxiety online as you do in person. It IS social. So be prepared for that, and again, be smart. Since the lockdowns, most of us have become adept at using Zoom. I recently recorded myself reading the first chapter of one of my books on StreamYard and sent it off to be uploaded on someone's site. It's also on my website. Some authors have become successful by reading their books aloud online. You can also do an online launch. Keep it short and advertise it to your friends and followers.

Submit to Anthologies. Many writers experience exponential success by joining with others in a themed anthology. When the writers get all their friends and their friends' friends to buy the book, suddenly it's on the best-seller list. Add that to your resume.

Choose Your Platforms. I know some successful authors who only publish e-books on KDP Select (Kindle Unlimited). They earn income from page reads and royalties and rarely venture out into the marketing arena.

Listen to your Intuition. If your inner guidance system screams, "Don't do it!" then don't do it. That sounds simple, but we often pressure ourselves into doing something because we feel we should and then pay the consequences.

Plan Ahead. If I've signed up for a day or weekend market or conference, I know the next two days I'll be exhausted. Introverts need alone time to recharge, so plan for it.

Trust the Universe. Characters appear as muses and ask us to write their stories. How can you say no? Write your book and let it go. Wrap it in love and trust that it will find its way.

ACKNOWLEDGEMENTS

First, big hugs to Metta Joy and the women who attended our psychic development and meditation classes. That includes Mary, Niloo, and Yasaman, who, by the way, designed and illustrated all the tattoo book covers for the Hollystone Mysteries. Later, Joy came to my first Muse workshops along with Tara, Sarah, Leisa, and Rhiannon. I couldn't have done this without you.

Many thanks to authors Marie Powell and Sionnach Wintergreen who beta read earlier drafts with keen eyes and open hearts, and wrote me such wonderful endorsements.

A big hug to Veta Lynne Murray who was my first spiritual teacher in Oshawa, Ontario way back in 1989. Lynne and I lost track of each other for twenty-five years and met again in the back rows of the auditorium at the Surrey International Writers Festival in October 2017. What synchronicity! Lynne continues to support my writing.

I need to thank my family, Gail, Tara, and Dakota for their support, and especially the little red-haired boy and Skaha who force me to go outside into the sunshine when I've been sitting far too long at my computer.

Finally, many thanks to Mickey Mikkelson of Creative Edge Publicity, and all the readers, writers, and reviewers who read and support my work. Many people have helped me over the years and I appreciate every last one of you. A shout out also to Indie bookstores and all the organizers of farmer's markets, book festivals, and writing conferences who put their time and energy into creating venues for writers like me and you to sell our books.

Blessings to you all.

Wendy

ABOUT THE AUTHOR

W. L. Hawkin writes the kind of books she loves to read from her home in the Pacific Northwest. Because she's a genre-blender, you might find crime, mystery, romance, suspense, fantasy, adventure, and even time travel, interwoven in her stories.

If you like "myth, magic, and mayhem" her Hollystone Mysteries feature a coven of West Coast witches who solve murders using ritual magic and a little help from the gods. The books—*To Charm a Killer, To Sleep with Stones, To Render a Raven, To Kill a King,* and *To Dance with Destiny*—follow Estrada, a free-spirited, bisexual magician and coven high priest as he endeavors to save his family and friends while sorting through his own personal issues.

Her standalone novel, *Lure: Jesse & Hawk* (2022) won a National Indie Excellence Award, a Gold Reader's Choice award from *Connections E-magazine*, a Crowned Heart

Review from *InD'tale Magazine,* and placed as a finalist in The UK Wishing Shelf Book Awards. Lure is a small-town romantic suspense story set on a Chippewa Reservation in the American Midwest near the fictional town of Lure River.

As an intuitive writer, Wendy captures what she sees and hears on the page, and allows her muses to guide her through the creative process. In an upcoming book, *Writing with your Muse: a Guide to Creative Inspiration,* she explains her writing process and offers tips and techniques to help writers get their words on the page.

Wendy needs to feel the energy of the land so, although she's an introvert, in each book her characters go on a journey where she's traveled herself.

If you don't find her at Blue Haven Press, she's out wandering the woods or beaches of Vancouver Island with her beautiful yellow dog.

If you enjoyed this book, please take a moment to leave a few words with your favorite retailer. Thank you.

Are you curious to know more about Lure River, Hollystone Coven, and W. L. Hawkin's latest news? Come by http://bluehavenpress.com, subscribe to Wendy's seasonal newsletter, and follow her on social media.

f facebook.com/wlhawkin

⊙ instagram.com/w.l.hawkin

g goodreads.com/author/show/16142078.W_L_Hawkin

in linkedin.com/in/wendy-hawkin-4321b2215/

▶ youtube.com/@wlhawkin/videos

www.ingramcontent.com/pod-product-compliance
Lightning Source LLC
Chambersburg PA
CBHW022124050726
47590CB00002B/389